Llama

Animal
Series editor: Jonathan Burt

Llama

Helen Cowie

REAKTION BOOKS

For Paul

Published by
REAKTION BOOKS LTD
Unit 32, Waterside
44–48 Wharf Road
London N1 7UX, UK
www.reaktionbooks.co.uk

First published 2017
Copyright © Helen Cowie 2017

Printed and bound in China

A catalogue record for this book is available from the British Library

ISBN 9 781 78023 738 1

Contents

Introduction

In 1558 a strange creature arrived in the Dutch city of Middelburg. According to contemporary reports, the animal, described by one writer as an 'Indian Sheepe, out of the region of Peru', was 'about two yardes high, and some five foote in length'. Its neck was 'as white as a Swan', its body 'yellowish' and its feet somewhere between those of an ostrich and those of a camel. The creature had arrived in the Netherlands via the port of Antwerp, and was the property of a merchant, Theodoric Neus, who subsequently presented it to the Holy Roman Emperor, Ferdinand I. Those who observed it estimated its age at 'not past four yeare olde' and reported that 'it was a most gentle and meek beast'. The naturalist Conrad Gesner included a striking image of the animal in his famous *Historia animalium* of 1563, under the title 'Allocamelus'.[1]

The animal that enthralled the inhabitants of Middelburg was a llama. It was one of the first of its species to appear alive in Europe, and just one of many new animals and plants to enter European consciousness following Spain's 'discovery' and conquest of the New World. Along with the armadillo, the anteater and numerous other previously unknown species, the llama and its close relatives the alpaca, guanaco and vicuña fascinated early modern scholars and forced them to revise existing systems of zoological classification devised by the Greeks and the Romans.

Baby alpaca, Chivay, Peru.

7

As a domesticated and potentially useful animal, the South American camelid also piqued European interest as a possible economic asset, operating by turns as a means of transport in the silver mines of Potosí, a source of high-quality wool and a producer of bezoar stones, much prized in contemporary medicine as an antidote to poison. The llama was thus a curiosity and a commodity, fuelling both the economy and the imagination.

In the years since Ferdinand I's llama arrived in Middelburg, llamas and alpacas have become much better known to Europeans. They have been used as beasts of burden in the Andes, farmed intensively for their wool and exhibited in zoos and travelling menageries. They have also emerged as popular pets, the hobby farm animal of choice for many British and American livestock owners. Today, llamas and alpacas are relatively common in the United Kingdom, Australia and the United States,

'Allocamelus', from Conrad Gesner, *Historia animalium* (1563).

where they are known for their haughty demeanour, woolly charm and propensity to spit when annoyed! In their native Peru and Bolivia they remain central to Andean culture, with alpaca wool providing a valuable export. Peru holds a national Alpaca Day every 1 August in honour of its most lucrative animal and Bolivia lobbied the UN (unsuccessfully) to make 2016 the International Year of Camelids. Llamas and alpacas may have become more familiar in the five centuries since the Spanish first encountered them, but they have lost none of their appeal.

My own encounters with camelids have been less dramatic than Gesner's first view of a llama, but no less memorable. In the process of writing this book, I have stalked llamas around Machu Picchu, tracked graceful vicuñas in the Peruvian *puna*, visited an alpaca fibre factory in Arequipa and watched alpaca judging at the Devon County Show. I have also examined pre-Columbian representations of camelids in museums and scoured Bradford in search of the (sadly now demolished) 'Alpaca Beerhouse'. My experiences have led me to greatly admire these handsome, spirited creatures and to appreciate their importance to Andean peoples past and present. This book offers an introduction to the wonders of llama anatomy and behaviour and traces the history of South American camelids from their domestication to the twenty-first century.

1 Alpacas Unpacked

All South American camelids belong to the genus *Lama*. There are four separate species: the llama (*Lama glama*), the alpaca (*Vicugna pacos*), the guanaco (*Lama guanicoe*) and the vicuña (*Vicugna vicugna*). South American camelids belong to the taxonomic order Artiodactyla (even-toed ungulates), suborder Tylopeda (pad-footed ungulates) and the family Camelidae. Andean animals are divided into two groups, *uywa* (domesticated) and *sullka* (wild).

Camelids originated in the Great Plains of North America. The oldest-known proto-camelid, a hare-sized, forest-dwelling creature called *Protylopus*, existed forty to fifty million years ago in the Eocene era. Between 24 and five million years ago, during the Oligocene and Miocene epochs, *Protylopus* evolved into *Poebrotherium*, an animal the size of a goat and with a longer neck than its ancestor. *Poebrotherium* evolved in turn into a number of different species, one of which was *Procamelus*, a still larger animal with the distinctive dentition and soft foot pad of the modern camel and llama. When a land bridge formed between North and South America approximately three million years ago, a descendant of *Procamelus*, *Hemiauchenia*, migrated to the southern continent, while another descendant crossed the Bering Strait and arrived in Asia. The latter gave rise to the Old World camel and the former evolved into the South American guanaco and vicuña. The original North American camelids disappeared during the Ice Age, around 10,000 to 20,000 years ago, at the end of the Pleistocene era.[1]

Lamas live high in the Andes, in elevated grasslands known as the *puna*. Vicuñas inhabit the highest altitudes, at elevations of 3,700 metres and above, while guanacos range from northern Peru to Tierra del Fuego and live in arid or semi-arid habitats from sea level to 4,000 metres. Wild vicuñas and guanacos live either in family groups (known as harems), as groups of young males or as solitary males. Family groups generally consist of a single alpha male and a group of three to five females, plus their young. Groups of young bachelors may be larger, ranging from just a few individuals to as many as sixty animals. Guanaco groups can be sedentary or migratory, depending on the quality of forage.

Guanaco family, Torres del Paine National Park, Chile.

When they are mature, solo males break away from male groups and challenge the alpha males at the head of the harems.

Llamas and alpacas exist only in domesticated form and can be distinguished from one another by their relative size, the length of their fleece, the shape of their ears and the position of their tails. Llamas are bigger than alpacas, have banana-shaped ears and typically hold their tails aloft when walking. Alpacas have long wool and spear-shaped ears and do not raise their tails. Llamas range more widely than alpacas, and have long been used to transport goods from the high Altiplano down to the Peruvian coast. Alpacas, used primarily for their meat and wool, thrive only at high altitudes, suffering malaise when brought below 1,000 metres.

The earliest evidence for camelid domestication dates back to around 4500 BC, though archaeologists disagree as to whether domestication occurred at one single site and spread out across the Andes, or whether it occurred simultaneously in multiple sites. The archaeozoologist E. S. Wing found camelid remains in Pikimachay Cave in Ayacucho, Peru, dating from between 4500 and 3100 BC. Another archaeozoologist, Jane Wheeler, reports a similar date of around 4300 BC for early camelid domestication at Telarmachay Cave near Junín. Teeth and bone morphology of these specimens, together with contextual evidence such as the presence of enclosure structures and fibre samples, suggest that the bones found in these locations belonged to domesticated llamas, rather than wild species hunted for their meat.[2]

The precise relationship between Peru's four camelid species has long been debated. Writing in the eighteenth century, the Jesuit priest Juan de Velasco confessed that he had seen llamas

An alpaca grazes in the Peruvian Andes. The animal's shorter stature, longer wool and more compact ears distinguish it from the llama.

and alpacas 'daily for many years', but still could not be sure if they were different species or merely varieties of a single animal.[3] The nineteenth-century French zoologist Frédéric Cuvier regarded the alpaca as 'a mere variety of the Llama, with the wool more amply developed'. He considered the vicuña the only distinct species, assigning it a different genus.[4] Recent molecular studies indicate that the llama is a domesticated guanaco and the alpaca is a domesticated vicuña.[5] All species have 74 chromosomes and are cross-fertile.

Camelids generally have a shorter lifespan in the wild than in a domesticated state. Guanacos rarely survive for more than twelve years, although elderly males of sixteen or eighteen have been known. The leading cause of death among guanacos is starvation, which accounts for over 80 per cent of all deaths in the Tierra del Fuego region. Hunting and mange account for additional fatalities.[6]

For llamas, the average lifespan is fifteen years, though some animals reach twenty. Llamas' teeth wear down in their late teens,

Pepito the alpaca investigates a miniature banana, Puerto Inca, Peru.

14

Keeper Conrad Ciferri brushes a handsome white alpaca at Central Park Zoo, New York, 1935.

preventing them from foraging effectively. The world's oldest recorded alpaca, 'Vomiting Violet', died in 2005, aged 29.[7]

All South American camelids are highly valued for their wool, particularly the alpaca and the vicuña. *Lama* wool is, in fact, technically hair, since it is hollow in the middle. It is extremely fine, soft and silky. Alpaca fibre measures from 20 to 35 microns, llama undercoat from 20 to 40 microns and guanaco wool from 14 to

15 microns.[8] Vicuña wool, the finest of all, measures between 12 and 14 microns and helps to insulate the animal against the cold and uv radiation experienced at high altitudes. Alpaca hair is said to be seven times warmer than sheep's wool.

Camelids come in a range of colours. Guanacos and vicuñas are almost exclusively fawn-brown with white underparts, while llamas and alpacas can be brown, black, white, grey or, more commonly, a combination of these colours, with a piebald or speckled pattern. This reflects the influence of thousands of years of domestication, which has allowed a wider range of hues to emerge. There are currently nineteen recognized alpaca coat tones and over a thousand different colour configurations.[9]

Alpacas are further divided into two types – huacayas and suris – according to the length and texture of their fleece. Huacaya alpacas have shorter, curlier hair and suri alpacas longer, finer and more lustrous coats. Suris are less common and more highly prized, commanding the highest prices.

Llamas are divided into ccaras and chakus. The ccara llama, the more common type, is used as a beast of burden, while the

A llama for all seasons: George the llama sports a headscarf in winter but dons 'sunglasses and self-satisfied expression' when the temperature reaches 26°C (80°F). Grant Park Zoo, Atlanta, 1958.

chaku llama is used for its wool. The chaku can be distinguished from the ccara by its thicker fleece and the hair over its eyes.

A llama walking. Photogravure after Eadweard Muybridge, 1887.

Unlike most ruminants, camelids do not have hooves. Instead, each foot has two toes, supported by cushioned, leathery pads and tipped with thick nails. The nails protect the feet, and occasionally need to be trimmed if they get overgrown. The pads allow llamas to have more sensation of the ground than hoofed animals, making them more sure-footed in craggy, mountainous terrain.

Lamas have special scent glands between their toes and on the inner and outer surfaces of the lower rear legs. The glands secrete pheromones, which scientists think may function as a form of alarm or for regulating body temperature. A third scent gland on the inner surface of the rear leg emits a smell that helps animals within the same herd to identify one another.

Living at such high altitudes, *Lamas'* bodies have evolved to cope with low oxygen levels. Camelids differ from all other mammals in having small, oval-shaped red blood cells. These provide a large surface area to which oxygen can adhere. *Lamas* also have high capillary density, which means that blood is delivered quickly and efficiently to muscle tissue. This latter feature is most pronounced in the vicuña, which has a very large heart for its body size, facilitating the rapid circulation of oxygenated blood. The vicuña's heart is almost 50 per cent larger than the average heart weight for mammals of a similar size, and bigger than those of other camelids as a percentage of its body weight. Llamas and alpacas have a heart rate of sixty to ninety beats per minute when at rest.

Lamas are equally well adapted for feeding in mountainous regions. South American camelids are ruminants and subsist

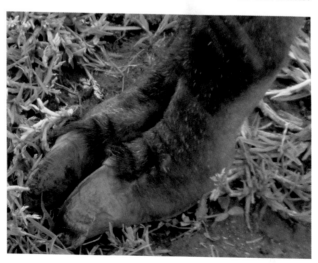

Llama foot.

A llama exhibits his long neck at Chessington Zoo, 1955.

primarily on *ichu* grass – a species native to the Peruvian highlands. Llamas and guanacos prefer the longer grasses while vicuñas prefer shorter varieties.

Alpacas appear to have the most catholic foraging behaviour, depending on the condition of the vegetation; in the wet season, they use tall grasses as llamas do, while in the dry season they move to feed on short grasses, forbs and sedges.[10]

To graze with maximum effect, camelids have a split prehensile lip, which enables them to grasp the grass easily and uproot it. They have no upper incisors, but rather a dental plate, like sheep. Mature males, however, grow long curved 'fighting teeth', which they use to bite off the testicles of mating rivals!

Once llamas have ingested their fodder it passes down the oesophagus into a three-chambered stomach. In the first chamber (80 per cent of the stomach volume), food is fermented and cellulose converted into digestible nutrients. In the second chamber some of the nutrients are absorbed. In the third – a tubular organ containing the gastric glands – food is broken down. Further digestion occurs in the small intestine, caecum and colon, where vitamins, minerals and water are absorbed and faecal pellets formed. Though not as efficient at storing water as camels, *Lamas* drink relatively little and can go without water for a considerable

A male guanaco attacks a rival, Torres del Paine National Park, Chile.

Black alpaca showing his teeth at the Devon County Show, 2015.

amount of time. The owner of the first living alpaca to reach Britain, the showman Edward Cross, reported that his animal

> did not once drink a tea-cup full of the water set before it, although chiefly subsisting on dry food, such as hay, beans and oats, with cakes and biscuits presented by the admiring visitors, and only occasionally supplied with carrots and green vetches.[11]

Lamas defecate in set areas, known as community dung piles, and their excrement, called *taquia*, is widely used in the Andes. The Incas used camelid excrement to fertilize their crops and, in dried form, for fuel.[12] Nineteenth-century Peruvians continued this tradition, using llama poo to power local industry. According to the British merchant Charles Ledger, without *taquia*,

> the large copper smelting establishments of Corocoro would be quite unable to exist a week . . . the Silver Amalgamating Works would be at a standstill, and . . . some two millions of human beings would be without fuel in a country where not a tree is to be met with for hundreds of miles.[13]

Today llama manure is used to fertilize another famous Andean export – the potato.

Humans are less fond of one of the llama's other qualities: its ability to spit. Spitting constitutes the animal's only real defence mechanism, and happens when llamas or alpacas feel angry or

A community dung pile.

Mrs Harriet Franklin poses with a llama at the National Zoo, Washington, DC, 1912.

threatened. Usually camelids spit at one another, asserting their position within the herd. On occasion, however, they will spit at humans, most commonly when touched or approached too closely. One of the first alpacas introduced to South Australia disliked being 'fondled and petted' and avenged unwanted 'caresses' by 'ejecting . . . a kind of steamy saliva' over her admirers, 'accompanying the impoliteness by a short, peculiar noise, something between a hiss and a cough'.[14]

Llamas can produce three types of spit: an air spit, a full-mouth spit consisting only of saliva, and true spit, which contains food regurgitated from the stomach. The latter smells absolutely foul, and also affects the llama, which will usually air its mouth for up to thirty minutes after issuing one of these stink bombs. The eighteenth-century French explorer Amédée Frézier claimed that llama spit was 'corrosive' and would leave a painful red spot on the skin.[15] This is not the case, but 'the stench is . . . abominable,

This unfortunate alpaca has just been spat on by one of his companions. Note the green stain on the side of the nose.

and it is difficult to get the disagreeable smell out of clothes, even after repeated washings'.[16] A llama will usually lift up its head and pin back its ears when it is about to spit, so if you see one doing this it is your cue to leave.

When it comes to procreation, llamas have some unusual physiological features. Female llamas and alpacas become fertile between twelve and fourteen months of age, though rarely breed until they are at least two years old. In Peru, adults will typically mate in August or September. Mating occurs kneeling down, in what is known as the 'kush' position. Male llamas are dribble ejaculators, which means insemination can take up to twenty minutes. Female llamas don't go on heat, but only ovulate after mating, typically within 26–42 hours of copulation. During the mating process, the male makes a distinctive guttural sound, known as 'orgling'.

A pregnant female undergoes a gestation period of around eleven months. In llamas, the typical gestation period is 350 days, while in alpacas it is slightly shorter, at 345 days. *Lamas* generally only produce a single offspring, though females are equipped with four teats and very occasionally give birth to twins. Births generally happen during daylight hours to protect the newborn animals from the cold Andean nights. Birth weights range from 10 to 11 kg (22 to 24 lb) for llamas and from 7 to 8 kg (15 to 18 lb) for alpacas. Camelids nurse their offspring, known as *crias*, for seven to nine months after birth.[17]

A llama airs his mouth after spitting.

A mother nuzzles her *cria* in an Italian circus, 1960s.

A female llama will usually only conceive once every two years, and may have five or six *crias* in her lifetime. Wild male camelids become aggressive during the mating season, but domesticated male llamas and alpacas are usually castrated by their owners, leaving only a few intact males to procreate. In Peru, these latter animals are known as *aynos*.

All South American camelids can interbreed to produce fertile first-generation offspring. The *huarizo* is the product of a male llama and a female alpaca; the *misti* is the product of a male alpaca and a female llama; the *paco-vicuña* is the offspring of a male vicuña and a female alpaca; the *llama-vicuña* comes from a male vicuña and a female llama; the *llamo-guanaco* or *llanaco* is the product of a male guanaco and a female llama; and the *paco-guanaco* comes from breeding a male alpaca with a female guanaco.

Camels can also interbreed with llamas, though only with human intervention. The world's first *cama*, or camel-llama, was born on 14 January 1998 at the Dubai Camel Reproduction Centre in the United Arab Emirates, using artificial insemination. Named Rama, the animal was the son of a female guanaco and a male camel.[18]

2 Sustenance and Sacrifice

South American peoples started to domesticate wild camelids around 6,000 to 7,000 years ago. Archaeological evidence of the presence of llamas and alpacas exists at important Amerindian burial sites, including at Chan Chan in Peru's Moche Valley. Camelid-shaped fetishes, figurines and ceramic vessels have been discovered in various pre-Columbian settlements. As the only livestock to be domesticated by humans anywhere in the New World, South American camelids fulfilled a role in the Andes equivalent to horses, cattle and sheep in Europe, furnishing ancient Peruvian civilizations with transportation, clothing and sustenance. They occupied a crucial place in the customs and world-view of successive Andean civilizations, shaping the diet, culture and art of the Moche (c. AD 100–800), Nazca (c. 200 BC–AD 600), Recuay (c. 200 BC–AD 600), Wari (c. AD 600–1000) and Chimu (c. AD 900–1470) people.[1]

Llamas and alpacas are particularly associated with the Incas, who dominated the central Andes between around 1400 and 1533. A highly advanced civilization, the Incas are remembered today for their sophisticated system of agriculture, their impressive road network and their culture of ancestor worship. From their capital in Cusco they amassed a large empire stretching from Quito in the north to the Atacama Desert in the south. Camelids played a major role in sustaining and expanding this empire, providing

Inca rulers with beasts of burden in peace and war, wool for clothing and meat for protein. They also permeated Andean religion, featuring prominently in Inca mythology.

The centrality of camelids to Inca civilization is evidenced by the care taken in naming and classifying them. According to Charles Ledger, the Incas called llamas 'Kaur-llacma' and alpacas 'paco'. 'The sexes could be designated in Quichua [*sic*] as urco, the male; china, the female'; thus an 'urko-kauri' was a male llama and a 'paco-china' was a female alpaca.[2] The wild guanaco was reportedly named 'for a neighing sound that it makes, because in making the sound it seems to say its name'.[3]

In addition to distinguishing between species and sex, the Incas also classified their animals according to colour. Describing

Hombre con Llama

Man with llama, Chimu culture, c. AD 900–1470.

Ceramic vessel representing a llama, Moche culture, *c.* 0–AD 700. The Moche often modelled their ceramics on local fauna and flora.

Pre-Columbian Huaco ceramics depicting sexual acts, in the erotic pottery section of the Larco Museum, Lima, Peru.

some of the 'sheep' sacrificed at the festival of Yutip-Raymi, the Spanish priest Cristóbal de Molina identified multiple gradations of hue, pattern and size, each of which had its own specific name:

> Those called *huacar-pana* were white and woolly. Others were called *huanacos*; and others, also white and woolly, were called *pacos-cuyllos*. Others, which were females with a reddish woolly fleece, were called *paucar-paco*. Other pacos were called *uqui-paco*. Other large sheep were called *chumpi*, which was their colour, being almost that of a lion's coat. Other sheep were called *Uanca-llama*, which were black and woolly.[4]

Multicoloured or piebald camelids were called 'mururmuru', transcribed by the Spaniards as 'moromoro'.[5]

The care the Incas took in naming llamas and alpacas was fully justified by the contribution the animals made to Andean life. In a pastoral society, high in the mountains, where crops were hard to grow and the guinea pig was the only other domesticated mammal, camelids formed one of the staples of the Inca economy. Without them, the Incas would have struggled to reach the pinnacle of civilization they achieved, or even to survive. As historian Karen Spalding has remarked, it is no coincidence that 'the homeland of Andean domesticated camelids' was also 'the cradle of the most powerful states to arise in the Andes'.[6]

Camelids contributed to Andean society in a number of ways. First, Andean peoples made extensive use of alpacas for their wool. Peruvian women were experts at spinning and both Inca men and women were known for their skill in weaving. The Jesuit missionary Bernabé Cobo, writing in the early seventeenth century, marvelled at the dedication of Indian women, who

Bags woven from cotton and camelid wool, late Nazca period, AD 440–600.

spin not only at home, but when they go outside, whether they are standing in one place or walking. As long as they are not doing something [else] with their hands, walking does not interfere with their spinning, which is what most of them are doing when we meet them on the streets.[7]

Fellow Jesuit José de Acosta was equally complimentary about Inca weaving capabilities, describing how 'all the work that they do is woven on both sides, and not a single thread or loose end can be seen in an entire piece of material'.[8]

To add colour to their clothing, the Incas created dyes from native plants and minerals. These included the red dye, cochineal (from beetles) and a blue dye extracted from a type of potato called *chapina*.[9] The dyes were applied to the wool prior to spinning and proved extremely durable. The French naturalist Alcides d'Orbigny admired the beauty and permanence of Inca dyes, which he examined on fabrics found in the tombs of Inca mummies in 1839:

With the art of weaving, the Peruvians possessed that of solid dyes, and we have found the remains of clothes which, though sealed in their tombs for at least four to five centuries, have nonetheless preserved their magnificent colours of reds and yellow.[10]

The Incas assigned different uses to different grades of wool, which in turn reflected strict social hierarchies. Cobo identified five different types of textile. The first of these, 'called *abasca*, was coarse and ordinary'. The second, '*cumbi*, was fine and valuable'. The third 'was made with coloured feathers woven into and fixed over the *cumbi*' and the fourth 'was like cloth of silver and gold embroidered in *chaquira* [beads]'. The fifth 'was a very thick and coarse cloth used for various rugs and blankets'. Clothing made from *abasca*, or llama wool, was worn by the lower classes, while fabrics made from *cumbi*, or alpaca wool, was worn by the nobility. The clothes of the Inca emperor 'were made entirely or partially of vicuña wool', mixed with 'viscacha wool, which is very thin and soft, and bat fur . . . which is the most delicate of all'.[11] As a sign of favour, the Inca would sometimes present members of the nobility with items made of vicuña wool. In this way, wool manufacture and dress practices reinforced and shaped class and gender identities.

As well as using camelids for their wool, Andean peoples consumed them as food. The flesh of both llamas and alpacas was employed to make a kind of dried meat known as 'charqui' (the origin of the modern term 'jerky'), which was first cut into 'wide, thin slices', then put 'on ice to cure'. 'Once the slices were dried out, they pounded them between two stones to make them thinner'. In this form the meat could be stored for an extended period of time without putrefying, and was frequently consumed in a stew.[12]

Alpaca and llama meat was often eaten after sacrifices:

To judge from the age profiles of camelid bones recovered from the Calchaquí valley, north-western Argentina, Inca feasts featured cuts of meat from animals in the prime of life, rather than from the aged animals often eaten in local communities once their working life was over.[13]

In the month of Coya Rami (September), for example, after thirty alpacas – all 'healthy, clean, without blemishes or deformities of any kind' – were sacrificed to the Sun in Cusco, the meat of four of the animals was distributed to everyone present, each person receiving 'a tiny portion' which they ate 'raw'. The *mamaconas*, or virgins of the Sun (young women chosen to serve the Inca), also made cakes called *sanco* from 'maize flour mixed with the blood from a certain sacrifice of white sheep [llamas]', which was brought out on 'large gold plates' and consumed as part of a ritual of allegiance to the Inca.[14]

The Incas did not drink the milk of llamas and alpacas, which they called *nuñu*, nor did they 'make cheese of it', for according to the Spanish chronicler Padre Blas Valera, the animals 'only have sufficient to nourish their lambs'.[15] Andean people did, however, use llama fat to mummify their dead and the skin of dead llamas and alpacas to make leather, from which they crafted slings, 'a kind of drum called the *huancar*' and sandals, called *usuta*. Bernabé Cobo reported that

the soles of this footwear are of untanned leather which is taken from the neck of their sheep [llamas] because the hide from that part is thicker than any other part of these animals. Since the leather is untanned, when it gets wet, it becomes as soft as tripe. For this reason they remove their shoes when it rains or when the ground is wet.[16]

Throughout the pre-Columbian period, llamas played a crucial role in transportation. In the absence of horses and donkeys, Andean peoples relied on camelids to carry goods, sending their flocks down to the coast carrying bags of wool, and bringing them back 'laden with maize, ají [chili] and pulses'.[17] Llamas were well adapted for this kind of work, climbing easily over the difficult mountain terrain and subsisting on the *ichu* grass that grew in the sierra. They could carry between 25 and 30 kg (55 and 66 lb) and cover around 3 leagues per day, though, if pushed too far, they would sit down and refuse to move, making 'cries very similar to the grunting of Pigs'.[18] The Incas used llama caravans extensively in their military campaigns, deploying them alongside human porters. The Inca general Quizquiz abandoned some 15,000 pack llamas in the eastern mountains after a battle in the first years of the Spanish conquest – an indication of the large numbers employed in this type of work.[19]

Given the vital role of llamas and alpacas in the Andean economy, it is not surprising that the Incas devoted considerable resources to farming them. The animals thrived best in the coldest regions of Peru, high in the Andes. They were reared 'in all parts of the Collao, and on the mountains towards Arequipa and the coast, as well as throughout Carancas, Aullagas, Quilluas and Collahuas'.[20] According to the Spanish conquistador Pedro Cieza de León, the Incas also 'made an effort to introduce flocks into areas where they were unknown as part of the indigenous economy, especially in northern Peru and parts of highland Ecuador'.[21]

The Incas managed their flocks carefully to ensure sustainability and fair distribution, reflecting the values of mutuality and reciprocity upon which their society was founded. Some camelids belonged to communities, some belonged directly to the Inca and some were set aside for the sun, to which they were sacrificed on a regular basis. 'Those belonging to religion and to

the Ynca were called *Capac-llama*, and the others *Huachay-llama*; which means rich and poor beasts'.[22] Every November the Inca conducted a census of 'state and temple' animals to estimate how many there were. The number of animals of each colour was recorded in *quipus* – knotted threads employed as a form of account keeping.[23]

This image from Felipe Guamán Poma, *El Nuevo corónica y buen gobierno* (1615) depicts a young girl tending flocks of camelids. Herding was typically a job assigned to adolescents. Drawing 85, 'The sixth "street" or age group, *qhuru thaski*, short-haired girl of twelve years.'

Padre Blas Valera claimed that the Incas divided their flocks according to the colour of the animals, so that 'if a lamb was born of a different colour from its parents, it was passed into the flock of its own colour' after it had been weaned.[24] Alpacas were sheared annually and their wool divided among members of the community, 'each getting the quantity he required for himself, his wife and children; so that all were clothed'. To guarantee the continued fertility of their flocks, the Incas refrained from killing any female, imposing a 'severe punishment' on anyone who did so. They also developed a novel method of treating a disease called 'carache' (probably scabies), burying afflicted beasts 'at once, deep in the ground' to prevent them infecting the entire flock.[25]

Guanacos and vicuñas were not farmed by the Incas, but hunted intermittently to secure their meat and wool. These hunts, known as *chakkus*, were organized by the Inca emperor himself and generally entailed surrounding prey in a large enclosure. As Cieza de León explained:

> Having assembled fifty thousand or sixty thousand people, they surrounded the plains and broken ground . . . making the country resound with the noise of their voices. Gradually they approached each other, until they formed a ring with hands joined, and in the enclosed space bounded by their bodies the flocks were detained and secured . . . Then certain Indians entered the enclosure armed with *ayllos* [bolas – a type of lasso], which are used to secure the legs, and others with sticks and clubs, and began to seize and kill.

Cieza de León estimated that 'as many as thirty thousand head' of vicuñas and guanacos might be killed during a single *chakku*.[26] Fellow chronicler Garcilaso de la Vega, however, claimed only the males perished in these hunts, for the Incas would release female guanacos and vicuñas 'after they had been sheared'. He also stated that the Incas kept *quipu* records of the number of animals caught and killed, and would only hunt in a particular region one year in every four, partly to conserve stock, partly because 'the Indians say that in this space of time the wool of the vicuña grows to its full extent'.[27] In this way, vicuña hunting was made into a sustainable activity, and the Incas managed the conservation of their wild camelids as carefully as they managed the farming of their domesticated counterparts.

Llamas and alpacas suffused Andean religion. Central to Peruvian agriculture, they assumed an equally pivotal position in the spiritual world of the Incas, often playing a mediating role between the people and their gods. Camelids figured prominently in pre-Columbian rituals and ceremonies, sometimes as sacrificial offerings, sometimes as objects of adoration in their own right. Writing in the nineteenth century, the British alpaca acclimatizer William Walton assigned them a comparable status to 'the white elephant among the Siamese and white cow with the Hindoos', both revered as sacred species in their native lands.[28]

Among the myriad ways in which llamas and alpacas entered Inca cosmography, the most visible was as victims of sacrifice. Llamas and alpacas were sacrificed regularly to the various Gods worshipped by the Incas. Some were sacrificed to the creator god Viracocha, some to the moon and some to the god of thunder, Ilapa. A llama was sacrificed daily in Cusco to the sun god Inti, to whose worship entire flocks were dedicated. Nineteenth-century archaeologist Mariano Rivero calculated that 'some two hundred thousand llamas were killed annually in honour of the Sun'.[29]

The kind and colour of animal chosen for sacrifice depended on the intended recipient and the time of the year. In the month of Capac Raymi (January), when Inca boys underwent an initiation ceremony, the camelids selected for sacrifice had 'long wool and stiff straight tails'. In the following month, Camay (February), the Incas sacrificed 'light brown' camelids, 'white from the knees down, with white heads'. In the month of Hatun

Puquy (March), during the rainy season, a hundred chestnut-coloured llamas were killed.[30] The vast majority of the llamas and alpacas sacrificed were males or sterile females, ensuring that the propagation of the species was not threatened by the high number of offerings.[31]

Bernabé Cobo gave a detailed description of camelid sacrifice at the major Inca festival of Capac Raymi, an event held to mark the coming of age of young Inca nobles:

> One hundred sheep [llamas and alpacas] were brought out with great solemnity. These animals were selected from among all those that had been gathered that year, and were healthy and without injury, with long wool and stiff

Incas worship the sun in this romanticized 18th-century image. Four llamas graze in the bottom left-hand corner. B. Picart, 'Le premier jour de la grande Fête du Soleil', 1722.

straight tails. The major priest of the Sun would stand up at this time, and making a reverent gesture first to Viracocha and then to the rest of the statues, he had the sheep led four times around the statues, and after this the animals were offered on behalf of the Sun to Viracocha, and after offering them, they were turned over to thirty Indians who were assigned to take them, and each day they sacrificed three of them. Therefore, at the end of the month, all of them would be gone because on some days four of them would be sacrificed.

Cobo went on to describe how, on the second day of the festival, 'six very old sheep' called *aporucos* were led out by six Indians carrying 'a load of maize and coca'. They were walked around the square for four days, 'with a special solemnity' and, on the fifth day, 'bled from a certain vein that is above the right front foot', this blood being used by the young men to smear on each others' faces.[32] The procession was headed by an Indian holding the royal banner, the *suntur paucar*, and a special llama called the *raymi napa* (ritual sacred llama), with a cloth 'similar to a red tunic over it and gold ear tassels'.[33]

While major festivals like Capac Raymi witnessed multiple sacrifices, individual llamas and alpacas were also sacrificed on a regular basis at shrines known as *huacas*. *Huacas* were local religious sites, often taking the form of unusually shaped stones, springs or mountain peaks. They were regarded as sacred by Andean peoples and honoured with a range of offerings, including coca leaves, cotton and wool. Llama fat, believed to have life-giving properties, was employed in healing and fertility rituals and frequently used in the worship of *huacas*. 'Whether used in offerings, healings or divination rituals, fat symbolized, and still symbolizes today, the essence of life and of vital force.'[34]

As well as carrying out sacrifices, the Incas performed several additional rituals involving camelids. In the month of Ariguaquiz (April), an old llama was tied up in the square of Cusco for the whole month and fed every day with *chicha* (a maize-based alcoholic drink), which it sometimes kicked over, in this way making an offering to the gods. In the month of Homa Raymi Puchayquiz (October, referred to as Uma Raymi Killa by some other chroniclers), if there was a drought, the Incas placed a 'solid black' llama on a 'flat plain' and abandoned it there without food until it rained. This was intended to elicit divine pity, for it was believed that 'seeing this animal suffer would cause the Sun to feel so sorry that he would make it rain'.[35] Colonial chronicler Felipe Guamán Poma illustrated this ceremony in his manuscript *Corónica y buen gobierno* (1615), describing how the 'black sheep [*sic*] helps to cry and beg for water through its hunger'.[36]

'Silver llama and alpaca', from the Islands of Titicaca, Bolivia. The llama with the red blanket probably represents the *raymi napa*.

Drawing 99, 'The tenth month, October: *Uma Raymi Killa*, month of the principal feast', from Felipe Guamán Poma, *El Nuevo corónica y buen gobierno* (1615).

Shamans, or 'sortilegos', also used camelid cadavers to predict the future. According to Cobo, Andean 'sorcerers' would

kill birds, sheep or lambs. Then by blowing into a certain vein in the [animal's] lungs, they said they would find signs in the lungs by which they would foretell what was going to happen. Other times for this same purpose they would burn sheep's fat and coca. By a certain fluid that

Drawing 329, 'Native Andeans sacrifice a llama according to the ancient laws of idolatry', from Felipe Guáman Poma, *El Nuevo corónica y buen gobierno* (1615).

appeared and by other signs that were seen at the time of burning, they said that they knew what was going to happen to the one who hired them.[37]

Garcilaso de la Vega claimed that the former ritual was particularly important during the feast of Capac Raymi, when the priests would open up a black llama or alpaca while it was still alive and extract its heart and lungs. It was considered a good omen 'if the lungs came out palpitating' and intact, and if, when blown into, they inflated to a considerable extent. If this failed to happen, 'cruel wars, sterility of crops [and] the death of flocks' were to be expected.[38]

On a more personal level, ordinary Andeans kept llama and alpaca-shaped fetishes in their own homes. Known as *conopas*, these objects were generally carried about the person and believed to bring good fortune. 'The most elaborate had an indentation or space on their surfaces (or backs) where an offering (often llama fat) could be placed'.[39] *Conopas* were usually made of porphyry, basalt, granite, clay or wood, and occasionally of silver or gold. As well as camelids, which were generally represented without feet, they could take the form of maize, potatoes, monkeys, parrots or lizards – plants and animals that also played an important role in Inca culture.[40] *Conopas* have been discovered in various pre-Columbian settlements across Peru, and were confiscated on a large scale by Spanish missionaries following the conquest in an attempt to eradicate idolatry; in 1617 three Jesuit padres found 2,500 *conopas* in the Chancay region alone.[41]

Alongside *conopas*, Andeans treasured small stones called *yllas*. Originally formed in the kidneys of camelids, these stones were often carried by the Indians for luck. They were associated specifically with the fertility of Inca livestock and used to ensure the reproduction of the flocks. They were also sometimes buried in the fields to encourage a good harvest of maize. So prevalent were *yllas* among Andean people that the Spanish missionary Pedro de Villagómez referred specifically to them in a list of common sins he compiled for the instruction of fellow Catholic priests (1621). Fearful that Indians were still turning to pre-Columbian deities rather than Christian rituals (see Chapter Three), Villagómez ordered priests to ask Indian parishioners whether they were carrying sacred stones about their person:

> Did you, or do you, have in your house or in other parts *conopas, zaramamas* [stones carved in the form of an ear of maize] for the increase of maize or *caullamas* for the augmentation of livestock, or bezoar stones which they call *ylla*, for the same purpose?[42]

Finally, llamas and alpacas were prominent in Andean mythology, playing a central role in how the universe was interpreted and understood. They featured in Incan myths about the creation of the Earth and shaped their perception of the stars. Following the Spanish conquest, for example, the priest Francisco de Avila was told the following story about a great flood that almost destroyed the world:

Inca *conopa*.

Figure representing an alpaca, Cusco, Peru, Inca culture, c. AD 1400–1533.

In ancient times, the world wanted to come to an end. A llama buck, aware that the ocean was about to overflow, was behaving like somebody who's deep in sadness. Even though its owner let it rest in a patch of excellent pasture, it cried and said, 'In, in', and wouldn't eat. The llama's owner got really angry, and he threw the cob from some maize he had just eaten at the llama. 'Eat, dog! This is some fine grass I'm letting you rest in!' he said. Then that llama began speaking like a human being. 'You simpleton, whatever could you be thinking about? Soon, in five days, the ocean will overflow. It's a certainty. And the whole world will come to an end', it said. The man got good and scared. 'What's going to happen to us? Where can we go to save ourselves?' he said. The llama replied, 'Let's go to Villca Coto mountain. There we will be saved' . . . So the man went out from there in a great hurry, and himself carried both the llama buck and its load . . . [A]s soon as the man had arrived there, the ocean overflowed.[43]

Llamas thus played a role in the Andean version of Noah's Ark.

As well as helping to explain Earth's history, camelids made their presence felt in Andean astronomy. Probably connected with the flood story cited above, the Incas had a constellation called 'Yacana', which was believed to be in the shape of a llama suckling a lamb. De Avila claimed that

Yacana, which is the animator of llamas, moves through the middle of the sky . . . [and can be seen] standing out as a black spot . . . [The Indians say that] in the middle of the night, when nobody is aware of it, the Yacana drinks all the water out of the ocean. If the Yacana failed to drink it, the waters would quickly drown the whole world.[44]

While Yacana kept the Earth's water in balance, two further constellations, Urcuchillay and Catachillay, were worshipped by Inca herders. The former, a multicoloured male llama, was believed to watch over domestic animals. The latter, Catachillay, was supposed to resemble a female llama and its lamb. This constellation was shown to Garcilaso by his elders, but was apparently difficult to discern for one not familiar with Inca astronomy:

They tried to show it to me, saying, see there the head of the sheep; see there that of the suckling lamb; see the body, arms and legs of the one and of the other. But I did not see the figures, only [some black] marks, and it must have been through not knowing how to imagine them.[45]

Like their European counterparts, the Incas saw animals in the stars and imbued them with power over events on Earth. Where European astronomers saw rams, goats and lions, however, Andean sky-gazers saw llamas and alpacas – the animals most central to their everyday lives.

3 Peruvian Sheep

In 1492 Christopher Columbus landed in America and claimed the continent for the Spanish Crown. Over the following decades, Spanish soldiers surged across the New World. Hernando Cortés conquered the Aztecs in 1521. Eleven years later, in 1532, Francisco Pizarro dealt a crippling blow to the Inca Empire by taking the emperor Atahualpa hostage in an ambush in Cajamarca. By 1572 the last Inca stronghold, Vilcabamba, had fallen and the final claimant to the Inca throne had been executed. Peru, like Mexico, became a Spanish colony, site for settlement, source of silver and crucible for evangelization.

The discovery and conquest of America represented a collision not only between two human worlds, but between two distinct ecosystems. Old World plants and animals flooded into Peru in the form of cows, sheep, pigs, horses and chickens. At the same time, New World species made the journey back to Europe, introducing Europeans to maize, avocados, pineapples and chocolate. Hungry conquistadors, faced with the prospect of starvation, experimented with a range of American animals as food. Physicians scoured the Indies for new medicines while naturalists and missionaries attempted to explain the discovery of animals and people whose existence lacked referents in the Bible. Llamas and alpacas, so central to pre-Columbian culture, played a key role in this process of exchange, functioning by turns as sources of food, clothing and transportation. Their fate illustrates in microcosm the philosophical, economic, spiritual and environmental consequences of the Spanish conquest.

When the Spanish arrived in America, they were confronted by a stunning variety of new plants and animals that challenged existing knowledge about the natural world. Whereas Old World beasts – even exotic ones like the rhinoceros and the giraffe – had long formed a part of European thought, the species discovered in the New World had no precedent in natural history writings. There were no anteaters or alpacas in medieval bestiaries and no sloths or tapirs in the works of Greek and Roman authors like Aristotle and Pliny. Without literature to guide them, the conquistadors, settlers and missionaries who arrived in Mexico and Peru in the first stages of colonization had to rely on their own experiences and observations to understand this new and unusual fauna. They had to figure out what these strange creatures were and how they fitted within existing systems of classification.

In the case of the llama and alpaca, Spanish writers typically equated the animals with three well-known Old World species: the sheep, the deer and the camel. They referred to llamas and alpacas as 'sheep of Peru' or 'sheep of the land' and drew direct analogies with more familiar creatures to convey what they looked like. The Italian sailor Antonio Pigafetta, in what is believed to be the first published description of a South American camelid (1525) – in this case it was a Patagonian guanaco – characterized the animal as having 'the head and ears of a mule, the body of a camel, the feet of a deer and the tail of a horse'.[1] Jesuit missionary José de Acosta described vicuñas as 'larger than goats and smaller than calves', of 'a colour not unlike that of a lion', while Pedro Cieza de León, a Spanish soldier serving in Peru, described llamas as 'as large as small donkeys, with long legs, broad bellies

'Sheep from Peru', in Pedro Cieza de León, *Primera parte de la crónica del Perú* (1553).

... a neck of the length and shape of that of a camel' and 'large' heads 'like those of Spanish sheep'.[2] A later document, the *Relaciones geográficas* for La Paz, stated that llamas were 'as big as year-old donkeys and formed like camels, except that they have no hump'.[3] All of these analogies conjured a kind of 'jigsaw-puzzle' creature, as readers struggled to imagine a woolly camel without a hump or a long-necked goat with a lion-coloured fleece.[4]

Given the difficulty of describing camelids verbally, it is not surprising that images also became extremely important in the study of American animals. The Swiss naturalist Conrad Gesner, as we've seen, included an image of the 'Allocamelus' in his celebrated *Historia animalium* (1563), though his engraving exaggerates the size of the animal. George Marcgrave and Willem Piso's beautifully illustrated *Historia naturalis Brasiliae* (1648) features both a llama and an alpaca in a special appendix on Peruvian camelids, while a very similar image (almost certainly copied from Marcgrave) appears in the Polish naturalist John Johnstone's *Historiae naturalis de quadrupedibus libri* (1657), positioning the 'Vervex alius Peregrinq' between two different breeds of sheep – the 'Vervex aliud' and the 'Ovis Arabica'.[5] These images were not only important in transmitting knowledge about previously unknown species, but reflected a change in the methods of natural history. Before the discovery of the New World, early modern natural histories had tended to recycle the writings of classical authors such as Aristotle and Pliny, focusing not only on the physical form and behaviour of animals, but on their philological and symbolic connotations – their appearance, for instance, in fables, or on the crests of the nobility. After the discovery of America, however, European scholars were presented with a whole host of animals that had no place in classical writings and no previous biblical or literary associations. Unable to populate their entries on these new species with historical detail, they were obliged to focus more on visual representations made, where possible, from direct observation of the living animal (Gesner's illustration was purportedly 'taken from the sight of the beast'[6]).This technique was later applied to Old World animals, too, enshrining anatomical illustrations as central to the evolving discipline of natural history.

As for living specimens, there is some dispute as to when the first live camelids arrived in Europe. According to the nineteenth-century historian William Prescott they arrived in 1528, when the future conqueror of Peru, Francisco Pizarro, returned to Spain after a preliminary foray into the realm of the Incas and presented the emperor Charles v with 'two or three llamas', as well as 'various nice fabrics of cloth . . . many ornaments and vases of

'Vervex alius Peregrinq', from John Johnstone, *Historiae naturalis de quadrupedibus libri* (1657).

gold and silver'. Charles reportedly expressed 'particular interest in the appearance of the llama, so remarkable as the only beast of burden yet known on the new continent', and greatly admired 'the fine fabrics of woollen cloth which were made from its shaggy sides'.[7]

Other sources contest this chronology, suggesting that llamas did not reach Europe until the mid-sixteenth century. A guide-book to London Zoo from 1829, for instance, stated that 'the first Llama that was seen in Europe was landed at Middleburg in 1558' by Theodoric Neus, 'and sent as a present to the Emperor' Ferdinand I.[8] This was the animal depicted by Gesner. Whichever account is correct, it seems certain that individual llamas and alpacas had appeared in Europe by 1600, though, as we shall see, it was not until the eighteenth and nineteenth centuries that they were transported there in significant numbers.

The Spanish did not just observe South American camelids; they exploited them as a valuable natural resource. Spanish settlers needed food to eat, clothes to wear, remedies for illnesses and beasts of burden to transport goods. Sheep, horses and other European animals would fulfil some of these requirements once they arrived in the New World, but in the meantime settlers turned to native species to meet their needs. As the most significant domesticated animals in America, llamas and alpacas were among the first to be used by the Spaniards, serving a variety of functions.

Firstly, like the Incas, the Spanish used llamas as beasts of burden, particularly in mining. According to Acosta,

droves of these sheep are commonly loaded into a pack train, and in these trains go three hundred or five hundred or even a thousand animals, which transport wine, coca, maize, *chuño* [dried potato], quicksilver [mercury] and every other sort of merchandise, as well as the best merchandise of all, which is silver; for they carry the bars of silver from Potosí to Arica, which is seventy leagues.[9]

By the early seventeenth century, 8,000 llamas were reportedly employed in transporting silver from the mines of Potosí in Upper Peru (modern-day Bolivia), playing a crucial role in the colonial economy.[10]

Alpacas were also used to carry goods, though their smaller size and stubborn temperament made them less useful for this task. Acosta claimed that

alpaca sometimes grow angry and tired of their burden and will lie down with it and resist any attempt to make them get up. When this fit of annoyance is on them they would rather be cut into a thousand pieces than move.

Llamas transporting bars of silver, from Theodore de Bry, *Americae* (1602).

A feather-clad Indian beseeches a prostrate llama to rouse itself. In the background, two men can be seen hunting guanacos with bows and arrows. P. Van der Aa, *Galérie agréable du monde* (1702).

From this comes the expression that they have in Peru, saying of someone that he has acted like an alpaca to mean that he has become sulky or stubborn or spiteful, for this is what alpacas do when they are angry.[11]

In *Americae* (1602), Theodore de Bry pictures a troop of rather surly-looking llamas/alpacas transporting loads of silver across the Peruvian sierra, one of whom has sat down on the ground and is being coaxed by his Indian driver to get up.

Neither llamas nor alpacas were ridden during the colonial period. On occasion, however, Spanish magistrates condemned Indian criminals or rebels to ride on the back of a llama as a form of shaming punishment. Judges generally selected 'Moromoro Sheep' for this purpose, as riding on a 'moromoro', or piebald, llama was considered a greater humiliation.[12] Felipe Guamán Poma depicts a naked Indian sitting on a llama and being whipped in his 1615 manuscript, *El Nuevo corónica y buen gobierno*.

As well as using Peruvian camelids to transport precious goods across the Andes, the Spanish valued the animals for their wool, which was seen as superior in softness to that of European sheep. Cieza de León described the wool of the vicuña as 'as good as and finer than that of the merino sheep of Spain'.[13] Acosta reported that

> [the Indians] have the habit of shearing these animals, and from their wool make coverlets or blankets that are much prized, for the wool is as soft as silk and very durable, and as the colour is natural and not dyed it is permanent. These coverings are cool and very good for hot weather; they are held to be very healthful for inflammations of the kidneys and other organs, tempering the excessive heat.[14]

Philip II apparently shared the general enthusiasm for the vicuña, importing vicuña wool for the covers of his bed![15] The king even attempted to introduce vicuñas to Spain to farm them, but was thwarted by their delicate constitution. According to Gaspar de Escalona Agüero,

Drawing 211, 'The administrator of royal mines punishes the native lords with great cruelty.' The punishments include making an Indian strip naked and ride on the back of a llama. From Felipe Guamán Poma, *El Nuevo corónica y buen gobierno* (1615).

> Don Philip the Second . . . desiring to get to know and maintain an animal that produced such precious wool, issued a decree in Peru ordering that some vicuñas be remitted from that kingdom so that he could have them in the [royal parks] of the Pardo and Aranjuez.

Officials obeyed the order, but the 'excessive heat of the fiery isthmus of Terra Firma' killed the fragile vicuñas before they ever reached Spain.[16] There would be further attempts to naturalize both the vicuña and the alpaca in the eighteenth and nineteenth centuries – also largely unsuccessful.

COREGIDOR DE MINAS
COMOLOCASTIGACRV

elmente alos caciques prencipales los corregidores y iueses copoco temor
delaiusticia con seferentescastigos sin tener misericordia por chosalos po

enlas minas   enlas

Whether South American camelids were as good to eat as they were to wear remained a matter for debate. Acosta sampled vicuña meat while in Peru, but declared that their flesh was 'not good'.[17] Cieza de León, on the other hand, pronounced baby llama 'better and more savoury' than Spanish lamb, while Antonio de Léon Pinelo described llama meat as 'rather sweeter than that of our Sheep, but very good, and to make dried meat, which the Indians call charqui, the best that there is.'[18]

The need to experiment with alien foods diminished once sheep, cows and pigs had been introduced to the New World, with mutton, pork and beef taking the place of exotic American foods. Some Spaniards had, by this time, developed a taste for camelid meat, however, and llamas and alpacas – or at least parts of them – continued to be eaten by Spanish colonists.[19] According to William Prescott, 'many a llama was destroyed solely for the sake of their brains – a dainty morsel much coveted by the Spaniards'. 'Cakes' were also made from camelid bone marrow, and candles from their fat.[20]

Finally, like the Incas before them, the Spanish employed parts of American animals in medicine. After gold and silver, new drugs were some of the most sought-after commodities in the Americas. Philip II dispatched the physician Francisco Hernández to Mexico in 1570 with explicit orders to study the medical properties of American plants. Other settlers – notably the Jesuits – also devoted themselves to studying New World pharmacopoeia, discovering botanical remedies like guaiacum (used to treat syphilis) and the febrifuge cinchona (from which quinine is extracted). Though generally less lucrative than their plant-based equivalents, animal-based medicines quickly found their way into contemporary herbals, providing relief for a range of conditions. Acosta, for instance, recounted how he was relieved of snow-blindness by putting 'a bit of vicuña meat, recently killed and running with blood' over his eyes.[21] Bernabé Cobo claimed that 'the water that comes out of a half roasted [llama] kidney' relieved the pain of earache, while Martín Delgar, author of a medical self-help book in the eighteenth century, advised 'using burnt llama wool to stop bleeding when removing teeth, to end nosebleeds and to dry out cuts'.[22] In this way, camelid products were incorporated into a European medical system, sometimes as a substitute for unobtainable Old World antidotes, sometimes in addition to the latter.

Of all camelid-based medicines, none was more highly valued than the bezoar stones found in the stomachs of vicuñas and gua-nacos. Believed to neutralize poison, bezoar stones were formed naturally in the intestinal tracts of ruminants and highly coveted in early modern Europe. They were already known to exist in the East Indies, in the stomachs of deer, and were first discovered in Peru by the soldier Pedro de Osma y de Xara y Zejo, who extracted them from 'a certain little sack' in the stomach of a vicuña. De Osma experimented with the stones and passed on his findings to the Seville physician Nicolás Monardes, who confirmed that they were a 'marvellous' antidote to poison, good for 'disease of the heart' and excellent for 'expelling and killing worms'.[23] Other writers offered further suggestions on how the stones should be selected and used, with Acosta noting that they worked best if powdered and dissolved in 'wine . . . vinegar [or] orange flower water', and the Peruvian Jesuit Antonio de Léon Pinelo recommending the use of green-coloured stones over ash-coloured ones on the grounds that the former consisted of 'phlegm' and the latter of 'bile' – a reference to the classical theory of the four humours.[24] Several thousand bezoar stones were shipped to Spain in the first decades of the seventeenth century, attesting both to their growing popularity and to their successful integration into Old World theories of medicine.[25]

Bezoar stones are particularly interesting on account of the manner in which they were discovered, for this tells us a lot about how sixteenth-century Spaniards appraised potential new medicaments and assessed their value as pharmaceuticals. Like the plants and animals they came from, New World medicines had no precedent in existing medical literature, so physicians and apothecaries had to find out about them from other sources. This meant doing one of two things: consulting indigenous people about the medicinal uses of native plants and animals, or relying on their own senses and observations.

The case of Pedro de Osma offers a good example of both methods. Osma, as noted above, discovered bezoar stones in the intestines of a vicuña he had just killed. He did not do this without assistance, however, for although it was his idea to search for the stones, he was initially unable to find them, and only managed to do so with the help of a young Indian boy 'of ten or twelve years old' who had been accompanying him. This child was reportedly later 'sacrificed' by the other Indians for divulging the information, illustrating the difficulties and perils of passing knowledge between cultures and the understandable reluctance of native Peruvians to share expertise with Spanish settlers.

As well as seeking the assistance of local people, de Osma also tested the properties of the stones for himself and sent Monardes a dozen stones through his friend, 'the rich merchant Antonio Corço', so that he could 'perform experiments with them'. The conquistador emphasized his personal experience of American nature as a means of enhancing his credibility, noting that he had spent 28 years 'travelling throughout the Indies'.[26] He also cited the experiences of fellow colonists who had used the stones to cure serious illness, among them Doña Catalina de Vera, sister of a local official, and father Diego Fernández Clerigos, a local priest. The emphasis here on personal experience was typical of the process by which sixteenth-century scholars sought validation for their findings and represented a challenge to book learning and reliance on the teachings of the Ancients. As Monardes himself stated, '[I will] only put down that which I have experienced and the effects that I have understood [bezoar stones] to have, and those that have passed through my hands, so that [my observations] may be given complete credit.'[27] This new concern with direct observation was part of a wider epistemological shift among early modern scholars which would ultimately give rise to the Scientific Revolution.[28]

If the discovery of so many new species in the Americas thus challenged the Europeans' powers of observation and description, it also posed important theological and philosophical questions that forced contemporary thinkers to re-calibrate their understanding of the natural world. How had these animals got to the New World? Why did they exist there and nowhere else, and why were none of them mentioned in the Bible? Of particular concern to contemporary thinkers was a question that may seem arcane to us, but which was of critical importance to a highly religious society: how could the presence of llamas, alpacas and other previously unknown animals be squared with the Old Testament story of Noah's Ark and the Great Flood?

One of the first writers to tackle this thorny issue was the Jesuit José de Acosta. In his *Historia natural y moral de las Indias* (Natural and Moral History of the Indies, 1590) Acosta questioned why certain New World animals had no direct counterparts in the Old World:

If those sheep of Peru, and the ones they call *pacos* and guanacos, are not found in any other part of the world, then who took them to Peru or how did they get there, since no trace of them remained in the whole world? And if they did not come from another region, how were they formed and brought forth there?

Acosta noted that some animals in parts of the Old World only existed in specific localities, for example elephants, 'which are found only in the East Indies'. He surmised that

> even though all the animals came out of the Ark, by natural instinct and the providence of Heaven, different kinds went to different regions and in some of those regions were so contented that they did not want to leave them; or that if they did leave they were not preserved, or in the course of time became extinct, as happens with many things.[29]

Just under a century later, another Jesuit, the scholar and polymath Athanasius Kircher (1602–1680), was still brooding over the precise contents of the Ark and trying to explain how so many different species could possibly have fitted within a seaworthy vessel. Preoccupied with the logistics of the operation, Kircher drew a detailed diagram of the Ark in his book *Arca Noë* (1675), showing with great precision how the accommodation for animals and humans might have been laid out. In light of this piece of imaginative engineering, the Jesuit reasoned that not all known animals could have been lodged in the Ark, for there simply was not space. To account for their presence in the modern world, he theorized that some animals must have metamorphosed from existing ones when exposed to the excessive heat of the Torrid Zone, or been produced as hybrids of surviving species (the giraffe, for example, was a fusion of the leopard and the camel). Kircher listed several New World animals that he believed were not on the Ark – notably the North American Bison, which he regarded as a monstrous cow, and the armadillo, which he thought had been formed from a tortoise and a hedgehog. This was an early attempt to solve a problem that would baffle scholars for centuries to come: the distribution of animal species across the globe, and specifically the origin of American animals.[30]

While scholars in Europe wrestled with the place of New World animals in the Bible, missionaries and priests in Peru faced the more practical challenge of converting the Indians to Christianity. Evangelization was a vital component of Spanish colonization, providing the moral justification for the conquest of the Indies. Indoctrinating the Indians in the Catholic religion was not an easy task, however, and, despite some superficial successes, many missionaries were disappointed to find that pre-existing religious practices survived in the Andes, blending with Catholicism to create a hybrid form of worship. Llamas and alpacas had been integral to Incan religion, so it is unsurprising that they continued to feature in post-conquest doctrine. Sometimes they did so in overt opposition to Christian teachings. More often, their inclusion seems to have represented a subtle fusion of Old and New World beliefs – a phenomenon known as syncretism.

'Internal view of Noah's Ark showing the animals housed in their compartments over three decks', from Athanasius Kircher, *Arca Noë in tres libros digesta* (1675).

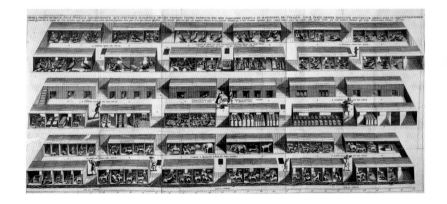

The survival of pre-Columbian religious rituals is plainly visible in the records of the Peruvian Extirpation (the Peruvian variant of the Spanish Inquisition), established in the early seventeenth century to root out suspected idolatry. In the province of Chinchacocha, for example, in the festival of Corpus Christi, the Indians processed through the streets with 'two live sheep of the land', which they subsequently sacrificed at the lagoons of Vrcocha and Choclococha.[31] In Uchupa Cancha an Indian named Juan Chapa and his wife María were summoned before the Extirpation for performing a rite that involved clipping the tops of young llamas' ears and offering them to the god Pata Caca. In the 1740s, an Indian named Domingo García was imprisoned by an extirpator for smearing 'llama's blood on the foundations and adobe walls of a new local church'.[32] In 1608, meanwhile, a woman from Puna named Barbola de los Reyes was convicted of bestiality after she confessed (under threat of torture), to 'copulating with a sheep of the land [a llama]'.[33] That such rituals were still being performed in the eighteenth century illustrates the longevity of pre-conquest beliefs, the limited impact of Christianity in the Andean world and the tendency to accommodate Catholic teachings within an older pre-Columbian world-view – a world-view that accorded camelids a central place.

Less overtly subversive, but still indicative of the distinctive local flavour of Andean Christianity, are the vivid frescoes that decorate Peruvian churches. Often painted by indigenous artists belonging to the Cusco School, these images depicted familiar biblical scenes, and at first glance appear little different from their European counterparts. On closer inspection, however, their Andean origin becomes apparent and old Christian stories are given a novel American twist.

La Moneda, Potosí, Bolivia, Painting of the Virgin Mary, c. 1740.

Take, for example, an image of the Virgin Mary in a church in La Moneda, Potosí. On the surface, this image looks orthodox

enough: here is the mother of Christ shrouded in a shining halo and flanked by her son and his father. If we cast our eyes down, however, we soon see things that do not appear in the New Testament. The Virgin's voluminous cloak resembles a mountain – one of the icons of Inca religion. The images of frolicking camelids, native birds and viscachas in the foreground have no referents in the Bible, while the crowned figure at the very bottom of the image with the emblem of the sun emblazoned on his chest looks very much like a representation of the Inca. This was a new take on religious iconography that skilfully blended the old and the new.

Other colonial frescos exhibit a similar form of syncretism, underlining the complex meanings of Christianity to native

Marcos Zapata,
The Last Supper,
c. 1750, oil painting,
in the Cathedral
at Plaza de Armas,
Cusco, Peru.

Mama
Huacco-
ñusłła.

Andeans. In Cusco Cathedral, a painting of the Last Supper shows Jesus and his disciples about to tuck into a guinea pig, or *cuy*, a local delicacy in Peru. In Acomayo, meanwhile, murals by the colonial artist Tadeo Escalante depict a variety of somewhat questionable Christian symbols, from a native lady flanked by a vicuña and several chinchillas, to a couple sacrificing a sheep while a llama, a horse and a shaggy-eared elephant look on in the background. A third image directly addresses the question of whether or not New World animals made it onto the Ark, portraying a pair of llamas approaching the ship's gangway, side by side with a couple of elephants (which they dwarf in size). This interpretation is shared by chronicler Felipe Guamán Poma, who depicts a llama in a sketch of Noah's floating menagerie,

Tadeo Escalante, mural paintings of 'The Mill of the Creation', Acomayo, Peru, early 19th century.

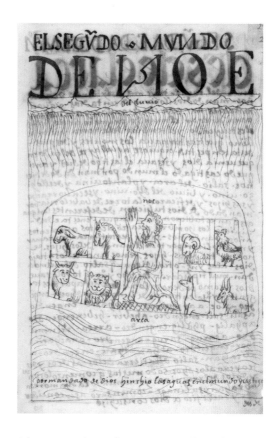

Drawing 8, 'The second age of the world: Noah.' A llama appears second from right on the lower deck. From Felipe Guamán Poma, *El Nuevo corónica y buen gobierno* (1615).

Modern Peruvian nativity.

alongside more traditional passengers such as a lion, a chicken and a cow. All of these images show how indigenous Americans created a unique form of Catholicism, imbued with their own pre-existing conceptions of the spiritual universe. For a Peruvian Indian who relied on native animals for food, clothing and transport, it was perfectly natural that llamas should be on the Ark, just as it was natural that Jesus's last meal should be roasted guinea pig.

If Peruvian camelids remained an important fixture in Andean religious iconography, they also soon earned a place in European art, where they functioned as a recognizable motif for things American. Very soon after the Spanish conquest of the New World, American animals such as the armadillo and the parrot became a form of artistic shorthand for the Americas, sometimes representing a particular region, but more often standing for the continent as a whole. The llama and alpaca, such a distinctive part of the Peruvian landscape, were among the most common zoological symbols. They operated as allegories for America and were to be found emblazoned on the cover of many a rip-roaring travel account.

A very early example of camelids being used in this way is a lurid scene in Lorenz Fries's *Uselegung der Mercarthen oder Carta Marina* (1525). Entitled 'Cannibals on the Caribbean Island', the coloured engraving depicts two dog-headed cannibals butchering a human torso with an axe. To the right, a third dog-man munches on a severed limb. To the left, a fourth cannibal stands over a hoofed, long-necked creature carrying a trussed human victim on its back. The image pre-dates the Spanish conquest of Peru, but the latter beast strongly resembles a llama. The scene as a whole typifies early representations of the Americas, which often featured cannibals, Amazons and other fanciful creatures.[34]

Slightly less sensationalist, but still rather fantastical, is Flemish artist Jan van Kessel's tableau *Amerika* (1664–6), which forms part of a series representing all four (known) continents. Van Kessel's work comprises one central image of a curiosity cabinet, surrounded by sixteen smaller canvases depicting the native fauna. One of these panels, 'Santo Domingo', features several peculiar-looking camelids, some with humped backs and some with horns, flanked by a gaggle of chimpanzees and a giraffe! Others show elephants, a unicorn, parrots and an enormous bat, as well as an armadillo and a tamandua. Painted in the mid-seventeenth century, van Kessel's tableau reflects Europe's continued fascination with the New World, and a love of the marvellous. The frightening images of cannibalism and monstrous beings have disappeared, but America's novel fauna clearly remained a source of wonder and inspiration for European collectors and artists.

As the fauna of the New World became more familiar to Europeans, camelids started to appear with more frequency in allegorical treatments of America, functioning as shorthand for the continent and its people. The frontispiece to Theodore de Bry's *Americae* (1602) sports two penguins, a naked Indian with feathered headdress and, in the centre at the bottom, a shifty looking llama, with more than the suspicion of a hump. Ulrich Schmidel's travel account (1599) opens with an image of the author seated on a llama and flanked by two natives, one of whom is holding a parrot, while an engraving by Juan Courbes in *The Kingdoms of Peru and New Spain* (1630) represents Peru as

Lorenz Fries, *Uselegung der Mercarthen oder Carta Marina* (1525), leaf XVI, showing dog-headed cannibals and a llama-like creature.

an Incaic figure clasping a tomahawk and accompanied by a llama (Mexico is represented by a female Indian with an eagle and a hummingbird). A fourth book, Francis Barlow's *A Geographical Description of all Countries in the Knowne World* (1657), depicts women from each of the four known continents alongside a native animal considered to typify the region: Europe is accompanied by a horse, Asia by an elephant, Africa by a lion and America by a llama. Exploiting stock images of the New World, all of these works reduce America to feather-bedecked Indians and exotic animals, stereotyping and simplifying the continent for a European audience.

Finally, towards the end of the seventeenth century, we find camelids represented in art produced in Peru itself, capturing elements of local colour. An interesting example of this is an anonymous oil painting of Lima's central plaza, dating from the 1680s, which features a vicuña and a 'sheep of the land' in a busy street scene. If you look closely, you will see that both of these animals have red numbers by their sides that correspond to a key

Detail from anonymous, *Plaza Mayor de Lima*, 1680, oil on canvas. A woman leads a llama on a leash (36) and a man whips a rearing vicuña (37).

in the right-hand corner of the picture. Many local fruits and vegetables are also labelled (for example, the pineapple and the potato), as is a native Indian woman. The fact that Peruvian species are identified in this manner suggests that the work may have been intended for a European audience unfamiliar with these animals and in need of clarification. The artwork was thus in part an educational tool, as well as an exotic curiosity from a distant colony.

Llamas, alpacas, vicuñas and guanacos thus served the Spaniards on multiple levels, carrying their goods, feeding their soldiers and functioning as a symbol for America. Their own experience of colonization, however, was much less positive. Victims of over-hunting, loss of habitat and disease, South American camelids were early casualties of the conquest and suffered a population decline comparable to the indigenous people of Peru. Their fate illustrates some of the wider environmental changes brought about during the colonial period.

Overhunting was the most visible cause of camelid depopulation. Llamas and alpacas were slaughtered in great numbers in the immediate aftermath of the conquest, predominantly for food. Prescott claims that, following the capture of Atahualpa in Cajamarca, 'the Spaniards . . . found immense droves of llamas under the care of the shepherds in the neighbourhood of the baths', which Pizarro commandeered 'for the use of the army'. The llamas were killed at a rate of about 150 a day, with the result that 'in four years more of these animals perished than in four hundred in the times of the Incas'.[35] Later, camelids were killed on an extensive scale to feed the growing population of Potosí. According to the Mercedarian friar Martín de Murúa, more than five hundred 'sheep of the land' were slaughtered in the city every week to provide food for the miners.[36]

Vicuñas also fell victim to Spanish voracity, in this case to secure their much-coveted fleeces. The Incas, as we have seen, had a long history of vicuña hunting, but did so in a sustainable manner. The Spanish, less conservation-minded and better armed, engaged in wholesale slaughter, severely reducing the vicuña population. Garcilaso de la Vega contrasted sustainable Inca hunting methods with the indiscriminate killing perpetrated by Spanish arquebuses, noting that 'guanacos and vicuñas are scarcely found, other than in areas where [the Spanish] have not been able to reach'.[37] Acosta concurred, remarking that 'since the Spaniards came too much license has been given to *chacos*, or vicuña hunts, and . . . their number has diminished'.[38] Concerned about the dramatic decline in vicuña numbers, the Spanish Crown imposed a five-year moratorium on vicuña hunts in 1557 – the first of repeated protection measures.[39] This had only a limited effect, however, and the slaughter continued largely unabated. The Spanish botanist Hipólito Ruiz described this new variant of the *chakkum* in his travel journal, noting the blend of New and Old World techniques:

> To carry out this kind of hunting, the natives fence in one or several hills and then climb up shouting, beating drums, blowing whistles, and snapping whips until they reach the summit or some other place previously agreed upon, usually in a corner where the animals cannot escape. In an open space or where there are not enough people, the natives make a low fence or cords a yard high and hang coloured pieces of cloth or wool upon it every few feet; this presents an impassable barrier to the animals. They also hunt on horseback or on foot with the libis, a rope $^1/_2$ to $^3/_4$ yard long and divided into four or more branches of the same length, with a round stone at each tip.[40]

In addition to the direct impact of hunting, there is evidence that llamas and alpacas succumbed to disease and loss of grazing land. Several early chroniclers spoke of some kind of sickness hitting the camelid population. Cieza de León reported that 'the cattle we call sheep' had been struck down by a 'great pestilence', while the Italian explorer Girolamo Benzoni, visiting America from 1541 to 1556, stated that there once used to exist in Peru 'a very great number of a kind of sheep as large as asses', but that 'not long ago a disease came over them like a leprosy . . . [and] destroyed nearly the whole of them'.[41] Pedro de Ondegardo,

'Chaco de Vicuñas', from *Trujillo del Perú*, vol. II, plate 113, c. 1790.

Drawing 328. 'The native administrator confiscates an elderly Andean's llama. "Hand over your tribute, old man", he orders.' From Felipe Guáman Poma, *El Nuevo corónica y buen gobierno* (1615).

corregidor (governor) of Cusco, claimed that many llamas and alpacas perished from a disorder known as 'carache', probably scabies.[42] It is unclear exactly which diseases wreaked so much havoc among Peruvian camelids, but it seems likely that they were introduced by the Spaniards, along with the fatal epidemics that killed horrendous numbers of the Indian population. It also seems likely that llamas and alpacas, like their human counterparts, were rendered more vulnerable to such illness by a decline in living conditions, as Indians lost grazing land for their flocks, Spaniards seized valuable livestock as 'tribute' (a form of taxation imposed on Indians) and newly arrived Old World sheep out-competed native camelids for food supplies.[43] Jane Wheeler estimates that 'both the human and the native domestic livestock populations were reduced by 80–90 per cent during the first hundred years of contact' with Europeans – a dramatic decline that continues to be felt today.[44] The llama, like the American Indian, was one of the victims of the so-called 'Columbian Exchange'.

4 Enlightened Llamas

In 1702 the Bourbon dynasty succeeded the Habsburgs to the Spanish throne. It inherited a stagnant economy, plagued by inflation and intermittent famine, and a vast American empire, which, though a potential source of revenue and resources, had grown increasingly autonomous of the mother country and was not fulfilling the supportive role envisaged for it by metropolitan ministers. Anxious to redress this undesirable state of affairs, the Bourbons enacted a series of reforms to improve the governance and profitability of the empire. Aimed at centralizing and modernizing the Hispanic world, these reforms began in Spain itself and were extended to the Americas during the reign of Charles III (1759–88). They included the introduction of the French-style intendant system in 1764, the creation of two new viceroyalties in South America and an overhaul of existing taxation models.

As part of this programme of reform, the Spanish Crown took a new interest in studying and exploiting the natural resources of the empire. To this end, the Bourbons founded new scientific institutions in Spain, funded a series of scientific expeditions to the American colonies and circulated instructions to overseas officials on how to 'select, prepare and send to Madrid all the curious productions of nature'.[1] Though aimed partly at furthering knowledge, eighteenth-century Spanish science was primarily utilitarian, seeking out plants and animals that could be exploited more efficiently to benefit the nation's economy. The minister of the Indies, José de Gálvez, for instance, keen to boost national industry, ordered the Viceroy of Peru to send rheas (ostrich-like birds) to Spain to 'promote in the Kingdom the teaching of working and composing plumes for plumages'. Another royal official, Pedro de Tagle, *oidor* of the Audiencia of La Plata, sent the king chinchilla skin from his native Potosí, believing that it might become a desirable commodity.[2] Already valued natural resources, llamas and alpacas featured prominently in this programme of enlightened economics, becoming

'Alpaca', from Étienne Geoffroy Saint-Hilaire and Frédéric Cuvier, *Histoire naturelle des mammifères* (1824).

candidates for trade, acclimatization and some of the earliest efforts at species conservation. Previously exploited without much foresight, camelids were now subjected to more rational management, as reformers in Spain and the Americas sought to maximize their economic potential.

The growing Enlightenment interest in natural history led, first of all, to the emergence of new knowledge about *Lamas*. Naturalists travelled to the Americas to study the animals *in situ*, learning more about their habits and geographical distribution. Camelids also arrived in Europe in increasing numbers, enabling sedentary scholars to view them at close quarters; the veterinary school at Alfort in France owned a llama between 1773 and 1778, which was examined by the famous naturalist Georges-Louis Leclerc, Comte de Buffon.[3] Scholars subjected living and dead specimens to close analysis, providing more accurate descriptions and illustrations of the species. The French zoologist Frédéric Cuvier dissected a llama's stomach to determine how the animal was able to retain water.[4] Another scholar, the Spanish botanist Hipólito Ruiz, observed the animal's distinctive mating technique, remarking that 'the penis of the llama is in a reversed position'.[5] Hazy ideas about camelid anatomy and physiology were replaced by detailed descriptions as close examination and careful measurement superseded conjecture.

Eighteenth-century naturalists were especially preoccupied with classifying American camelids and defining their relationship with other animals. Despite their superficial similarity to sheep, most scholars now believed that llamas and alpacas were a branch of the camel family and shared some of the characteristics of the Arabian species. They disagreed, however, over the number of distinct camelid species in South America, and how they related to one another. Were llamas, alpacas, vicuñas and

'La vigogne', from Georges-Louis Leclerc, Comte de Buffon, *Histoire naturelle* (1749–88), vol. XXXII, plate 5, p. 95.

guanacos separate species, or were they variants of a single animal? Buffon, who had seen a llama and a vicuña, concluded that there were three species: the llama, the alpaca and the vicuña.[6] Chilean Jesuit Juan Ignacio Molina, on the other hand, identified five: the llama, the alpaca, the vicuña, the guanaco and the chilihueque, an animal exclusive to Chile.[7] Unable to examine all these purported variants at once, naturalists in the eighteenth century failed to categorically resolve the varieties issue. The classification question would remain open until the twentieth century.

Spanish interest in llamas went beyond a mere quest for knowledge. More important was a growing awareness of the economic value of American camelids and a desire to maximize their use. This was particularly critical in the case of the vicuña, whose silken wool was used in Spain to manufacture luxury scarves, gloves, stockings, hats, sheets and handkerchiefs.[8] To meet the growing consumer demand, thousands of vicuñas were killed every year and their skins shipped to Europe. In January 1804 the frigate *Inni* left Buenos Aires for Hamburg carrying '3250 lbs of vicuña wool and 3194 of guanaco wool'; in August the same year the frigate *Nuestra Señora de la Regla* left Montevideo for Cádiz carrying '143 sacks of vicuña wool'.[9] It has been estimated that 'an average of 20,410 vicuña skins per year was exported from the port of Buenos Aires . . . in the eighteenth century'.[10]

The rapid growth in the vicuña wool trade was an economic boon to Spain, prompting government action to promote its continuation and expansion. Firstly, concerned that the wild vicuña was being over-exploited, the Spanish Crown issued orders in 1768, 1777 and 1789 to regulate the hunting of the animals in Upper Peru (modern-day Bolivia). These orders were intended to reduce the number of vicuñas killed for their wool and to encourage the less destructive practice of shearing the animals after capture. The 1777 order, for example, stipulated that *corregidors* (royal officials) in the Audiencia of Charcas must prohibit the Indians from 'killing the vicuñas in those hunts that of their own accord or at the bidding of their priests or corregidors they often engage in'. They must also oversee *chakkus* to ensure that the animals, if caught, were shorn and released. The enactment of these measures represented an attempt to protect an animal that was being rapidly 'annihilated' by overhunting.[11]

Jacques-Laurent
Agasse, *Vicuñas*,
1831, oil on canvas.

As well as attempting to preserve vicuñas in America, the Crown also tried to naturalize them in Europe. Surviving correspondence

in the Archive of the Indies in Seville reveals a steady stream of letters on the subject of camelid acclimatization, as ministers in Spain sent out orders to overseas officials and colonial bureaucrats recorded their efforts to fulfil them. On 22 February 1768, for instance, the minister of the Indies issued an order requesting that some vicuñas be sent to Spain from Peru. This elicited a reply from the viceroy of Peru the following July, reporting that he had

> succeeded in recent days in collecting three 'carneros' that are called 'de la tierra' [llamas] and a vicuña (many of the latter having died of a disease that often afflicts them . . .) which will be sent [to Spain] on the ship *San Miguel*.

A further letter from the viceroy, dated 1770, expressed doubts about the vicuñas' ability to withstand 'the heat that is experienced in sailing through the tropics', while assuring the minister of the Indies that the utmost effort was being made to ensure their

Vicuña and camel. Copper engraving print from the 1790s.

successful remission. A subsequent letter from 1772 reported the dispatch of 'three vicuñas and a guanaco' – the only survivors among the 'many that have perished, notwithstanding the care that has been taken of them'. The last reference to the vicuñas records their arrival in Cádiz aboard the ship *San Lorenzo* and the frigate *Santa Rosalia*. One of the animals 'died en route [to Madrid]'. Another was placed in the Casa del Campo, one of Charles III's royal palaces.[12]

Alpaca acclimatization was slightly more successful, though here political rather than environmental constraints proved debilitating. In 1802, prompted by advice from her scientists and ministers, the Empress Joséphine Bonaparte solicited a flock of alpacas for display at her residence at Malmaison, near Paris. Spain was then in alliance with France, so Charles IV's chief minister, Manuel de Godoy, arranged for 36 llamas, alpacas, guanacos and vicuñas to be collected in Buenos Aires and shipped to Europe. The animals arrived at the Spanish port of Cádiz in 1808, and the surviving nine (a pregnant llama, two female vicuñas, three mixed-race alpaca-vicuñas and three male alpacas) were installed in the acclimatization garden at Sanlúcar de Barrameda. Unfortunately the timing could not have been worse, for at this moment Franco-Spanish relations broke down, Godoy was ousted in a palace coup and Napoleon's army invaded Spain. With the export of the alpacas to France aborted, the Spanish quickly lost enthusiasm for the experiment and the intendant of Sanlúcar de Barrameda, Don Francisco de Theran, was forced to call on the governor of Cádiz to prevent angry locals from 'throw[ing the animals] into the sea'! According to the Spanish naturalist Mariano de la Paz Graells, the camelids were ultimately destroyed by 'the people', in a show of contempt for the 'hated mandarin' Godoy. Another source, however, claims that they were still alive when Marshal Soult's French army arrived in Andalusia, and were visited by the naturalist Jean-Baptiste Bory de Saint-Vincent.[13] Either way, the outbreak of the Peninsular War confounded the naturalization project, scuppering the long-term goal of acclimatizing the alpaca in Iberia.

While the Spanish were attempting to acclimatize alpacas in Europe, Spain's American subjects were also taking a renewed interest in Peruvian camelids. Inspired by the same theories of agricultural improvement as their contemporaries in Iberia, Spanish Americans pushed to domesticate the vicuña and the guanaco and to make the farming of llamas and alpacas more efficient. Where the Spanish Crown promoted reforms that would benefit the empire as a whole, however, Spanish Americans prioritized schemes that would benefit their respective homelands, promoting local industries at a time when the Spanish were trying to demote the colonies to producers of raw materials.

The first stirrings of American interest in agricultural reform appeared in the late eighteenth century and focused primarily on the vicuña. Writing in 1776, the Chilean Jesuit Molina advocated domesticating the latter animal, whose wool was used to make 'beautiful handkerchiefs, stockings, gloves, hats, etc.' Molina also favoured domesticating the guanaco, whose fleece was used to make sombreros and whose flesh tasted 'as good as veal'.[14] Thirty years later, a contributor to the Argentine periodical *El Semanario de agricultura, industria y comercio* outlined a similar scheme in which he proposed breeding the vicuña with llamas, alpacas and even domestic sheep to create a superior blend of wool. Convinced that good husbandry and the right climate were important for the vicuña's survival, the writer suggested conducting the breeding experiment in the Andean province of Salta and enlisting local Indians as shepherds. He attributed previous failures at vicuña domestication to rearing the animals in an

Camelus Huanacus Mol.

Parkinson del.   *J. C. Bock. sc*

overly hot climate and feeding them on a diet of bread, cake and chocolate.[15]

Another American to take an interest in camelids – specifically vicuñas – was the botanist-astronomer Francisco José de Caldas. Writing in May 1810, when Spanish America was on the brink of independence, Caldas addressed a memoir to the Real Consulado de Comercio de Cartagena in which he proposed naturalizing the vicuña in his native New Granada (modern-day Colombia, Venezuela and Ecuador). Caldas suggested that the Consulado should fund the purchase and relocation of one thousand of the animals, which he estimated would cost 2,500 pesos. He also urged patriots in his hometown of Popayán to raise a subscription to finance

the transport of a further thousand vicuñas to the mountains of 'Jasuay, Chimborazo, Cotopaxi [and] Pichincha'. Aware that vicuñas often perished when removed from their native *puna*, Caldas recommended shipping the animals to Guayaquil and allowing them to recuperate on the hills of Mount Chimborazo for several weeks before their final removal to Bogotá, Neiva and Santa Marta. Farmed and properly cared for, the vicuña would quickly reproduce in the colony, preserving the species from the 'cruel butcheries' inflicted upon it by ignorant Peruvian Indians. As Caldas put it,

> I am persuaded that the Patria [New Granada] would watch with pleasure the multiplication of the vicuña, adding one more species to the domesticated animals of this family, which is today wild in its country of birth, and New Granada would give an example of industry and economy to [the people of] Peru.[16]

Here, then, we see an example of inter-colonial rivalry, as a naturalist from one colony proposed appropriating a species native to another and managing it in a more 'rational' and sustainable way.

Unfortunately, as in Spain, none of these plans came to fruition. Molina was forced to leave Chile in 1767, when the Spanish Crown expelled the Jesuits from its dominions, while Caldas was executed by royalist troops during the wars of Spanish American independence. Despite their failure, however, the existence of such schemes reveals how the doctrine of agricultural 'improvement' spread beyond Spain to its American colonies and highlights the emergence of differing opinions within the empire as to the most effective use of the animal and who was best qualified to farm it. For the Spanish Crown, the emphasis was on bringing vicuñas to Spain and domesticating them there, using

'Huanaco', from *Trujillo Del Perú*, vol. VI, plate 4, c. 1790.

the latest European knowledge and technology. For Americans like Molina and Caldas the priority was making camelids serve the needs of individual colonies and taking advantage of more localized expertise. Though not necessarily evidence of a desire on the part of the colonies to break away from Spain, these internal differences reflect the rise of creole patriotism and the growing self-sufficiency of Spain's American territories – something the Bourbon Reforms were intended to counteract.

Spanish rule ended in 1826, but interest in llamas remained strong. In Peru and Bolivia, the natural homelands of these animals, the focus was on making the most of a precious natural resource and keeping it out of the clutches of rival nation states. In other South American nations (and beyond), agricultural reformers concentrated on naturalizing llamas, alpacas and vicuñas in their respective territories, breaking the Peruvian monopoly. In both cases, the tools used were government decrees and applied science.

Always a valued commodity, alpaca wool became an increasingly important export for Peru after independence, thanks to a growing demand for the material in Europe. Throughout much of the nineteenth century, alpacas were raised by Indian communities in the southern highlands of Peru and their fleeces purchased by British merchants, who opened trading houses in the port city of Arequipa and toured the sierra in search of the best prices. Along with sugar, guano and cotton, alpaca wool became one of Peru's most important exports, rising in value from £122,000 per year in 1845–9 to a peak of £489,000 per year in 1870–74.[17] The advent of new machinery in the Industrial Revolution made it possible to manufacture alpaca goods in a much higher volume, providing Peruvian herders with a ready market for their fleeces. A large quantity of wool was also consumed within Peru itself to make 'clothing, bedding, ponchos, sacks, bags, rugs and carpets'.[18]

Though less lucrative than alpacas, llamas also remained important economically, functioning as pack animals in mountainous regions and servicing Peru's other industries. According to the British wool merchant Charles Ledger, over a million llamas were employed in Peru and Bolivia in the 1850s and '60s, with 'some 800,000' animals used annually to carry 'wool, ores, metals, charcoal and provisions to the cities of the coast' and '830,000 or a million more' used in 'the carriage of grain to the upper lands'. A further 400,000 to 500,000 were 'continually employed conducting silver ores to the amalgamating establishments from the [silver] mines'.[19] Without llamas, Peruvian mining and agriculture would have struggled and Peru's economy would have ground to a halt.

Aware of the economic importance of camelids, Peruvians took steps to safeguard this zoological asset. First, following the Spanish example, measures were put in place to protect the vulnerable vicuña. As early as 1827, just three years after Peru secured its independence, the liberator Simón Bolívar issued a law prohibiting the killing of vicuñas for their wool.[20] Eighteen years later, in 1845, the Peruvian government replaced this order with a more comprehensive framework of legal protection, designed not only to prevent overhunting of vicuñas, but to maintain the nation's monopoly over alpacas. The new law stipulated that 'the exportation of live vicuñas and alpacas to foreign countries' was 'absolutely prohibited'; that earlier Spanish decrees banning the killing of vicuñas would be reinstated; and that the authorities would prosecute anyone found continuing the 'barbarous custom' of killing vicuñas in 'traps' or 'with dogs'. To ensure that no offenders could 'plead ignorance' of the law, the government ordered that its provisions be read out by priests to their parishioners on 'four

1852.   42.

consecutive Sundays', reaching even the illiterate masses of the sierra.[21] Further decrees in 1851 and 1868 reinforced the export ban, outlawing 'the removal from Peruvian territory of alpacas and vicuñas, and of any species of animal that proceeds from the crossing of the two races'.[22]

While the Peruvian authorities moved to protect existing resources, one patriotic citizen turned to science and animal husbandry in a bid to domesticate the vicuña. Stationed in the remote village of Macusani, high in the Peruvian *puna*, the parish priest Juan Pablo Cabrera combined his day job of ministering to the local Indians with an innovative project to interbreed the vicuña with the alpaca. After 21 years of experimenting, the persistent clergyman finally succeeded in breeding fourteen vicuña-alpaca hybrids, born of vicuña mothers and an alpaca father. The mixed-race animals possessed the chestnut-coloured 'snouts, ears and neck' of their vicuña mothers and the

'The Mêlée: Scene in "Aparoma"', April 1857, *Annotated watercolour sketches by Santiago Savage, 1857–1858, being a record of Charles Ledger's journeys in Peru and Chile.*

A Peruvian *chakku*, c. 1850.

97

white bodies of their alpaca father, producing a wool with the silken texture of the vicuña and the light shade of the alpaca (and therefore easier to dye). A single 'coffee-coloured' male was castrated to prevent him from breeding with his white siblings. The Peruvian government expressed great hopes that the experiment would constitute 'the fertile germ of an incalculable treasure for our backward country', rewarding Cabrera for his efforts by giving him a special medal and paying for his portrait to be placed in the National Museum in Lima, 'so that this benefactor of Peru is known to his compatriots'. To consolidate the domestication process, the government offered lifetime exemption from the *contribución indígena* (a form of head tax) to 'any Indian who presents to the Governor of his District ten perfectly tame female vicuñas along with a male of the same species or a male alpaca'.[23]

At the same time as the Peruvians were trying to improve and conserve their native camelids, other nations took steps to

Shearing alpacas in the Andes, 1875, woodcut.

appropriate them, flouting the 1845 export ban. The British and the French took the lead in alpaca acclimatization (see Chapter Five), but Spain also got in on the act, importing a small flock in 1857. Smuggled out of Peru by the French explorer Eugene Roehn, the flock of thirteen animals was shipped first to Cuba, re-embarked for Cádiz by the Havana Sociedad Económica de Amigos de País (Economic Society of the Friends of the Country) and transported by sea and train to Madrid. Though two of the animals died en route and another male was killed in a fight, the remaining alpacas arrived 'safe and sound after a journey of several thousand leagues' and soon started to breed. Mariano de la Paz Graells, director of Madrid's newly founded Jardín Zoológico de Aclimatación, congratulated himself on the acquisition of a

'Carnival time at Puno, Peru', c. 1890.

new and useful animal, sending photographs and wool samples to his French colleague Isidore Geoffroy Saint-Hilaire.[24]

While Cuban patriots helped to procure alpacas for Spain, the Uruguayan government worked to naturalize them in the Pampas. A Montevidean society for the acclimatization of llamas and alpacas was formed in 1864 to raise money for the project, and a flock of the animals was purchased by the society from the Italian Enrique Vigo, who had succeeded in smuggling them out of Bolivia. Vigo offered to transport the alpacas to Uruguay but died before the operation could be carried out. In 1867, however, another individual, Miguel Alviña, was contracted by the society to take his place, transporting the animals through the Argentine provinces of Jujuy, Salta, Catamarca, Córdoba and Santa Fe to avoid the battlefields of the Paraguayan War (1864–70). The alpacas' safe arrival was greeted with great excitement in Uruguay, which hoped to become 'the point of departure for the entire world of the Alpaca and the Llama and their magnificent products'. Just as the Peruvian government had rewarded Father Cabrera's achievement with a portrait in the National Museum, one Uruguayan, Augusto Fauvety, urged the government of Uruguay to commemorate Alviña's efforts with a statue, recognizing his role as a 'benefactor of humanity'.[25] As in Peru, alpaca appropriation and improvement were closely associated with economic prosperity and national honour.

As the above cases demonstrate, camelids were not only valuable economic assets in Spanish America, but occupied an important symbolic role as emblems of local and national identity. In the early colonial period, as we saw in Chapter Three, llamas and alpacas were often used allegorically as shorthand for America as a whole. In the eighteenth and nineteenth centuries they assumed a stronger regional significance, standing for individual nations rather than an entire continent. Llamas had particular resonance in Peru and Bolivia, where they formed part of a wider movement to celebrate the region's pre-Columbian heritage.

The first direct associations between creole patriotism and the natural world came in the late eighteenth century against the backdrop of a wider scholarly debate about New World fauna and flora. This debate was initiated by the French naturalist Georges-Louis Leclerc, Comte de Buffon, who claimed that the New World was colder and more humid than the Old World, and its fauna, correspondingly, smaller and weaker.[26] It was intensified by the Prussian philosopher Cornelius de Pauw, who alleged that the 'lions and tigers' of America were 'bastardized, small, pusillanimous and a thousand times less dangerous than those of Asia and Africa', while animals like the sloth and the anteater were ugly and deformed.[27]

Understandably angry about these slurs on their homelands, Americans summoned evidence to disprove them, pointing, among other things, to the beauty and versatility of the continent's camelids. The Chilean Molina argued that the llama and alpaca

Camelids often appear on coins and stamps. Here we can see a Bolivian coin from 1852, a Peruvian coin from 1850 and a Peruvian stamp from the 1870s.

The Peruvian coat of arms features a vicuña, a cinchona tree and a horn of plenty.

were much prettier than the Old World camel, 'the neck more upright and better proportioned . . . the back straighter . . . the legs better crafted and much more agile and the pelage longer, softer and more like wool', with the result that 'the camel is a monster in comparison to our quadrupeds'.[28] Another naturalist, the New Granadan Caldas, lavished praise on the graceful vicuña, describing its wool as 'the silk' of America; a third, the Peruvian physician Hipólito Unánue, extolled the elegance of American camelids, whose eyes were 'so beautiful and gleaming' that any woman would be proud to own them.[29] These comments formed part of a larger defence of America that sought to show that the

Challapaseños.

continent's climate and fauna were equal, or indeed superior, to those of the Old World.

After independence, the symbolic value of the alpaca was felt more acutely as the former Spanish colonies struggled to establish distinctive national identities. Keen to endow their newly created nation states with a sense of continuity and antiquity, creole elites in countries like Mexico and Peru often celebrated their pre-conquest heritage, mustering their Amerindian 'ancestors' and natural treasures as symbols for, and precursors of, their respective nations.[30] Llamas and alpacas featured prominently in this new national iconography, gracing flags, crests and regional artworks. The first Bolivian coat of arms (1826) featured an alpaca 'to represent the animal kingdom', along with 'an emblem of Potosí in a golden field, to represent the mineral wealth'.[31] Its Peruvian counterpart featured a vicuña, flanked by an Incaic sun, a horn of plenty and a cinchona tree (cinchona bark is used to

'Bolivian Alpaca Herders', Melchor Mercado, 'Republica de Oruro', c. 1850.

103

Mariano Benlliure's statue of José de San Martín features an accidental llama on the head of *madre patria*.

make the anti-malarial drug quinine), a design remaining on the country's flag to this day. Camelids also appeared regularly on coins and stamps – another site of national self-representation – as well as in art and sculpture.

One more unusual instance of a llama gracing the national pantheon occurred in 1921, when Peru commissioned a statue of General José de San Martín to celebrate the centenary of independence. Inspired by the traditional iconography of enlightenment, the Peruvian buyers stipulated that the statue should feature a female figure (*madre patria*), crowned with a 'votive flame' (*llama votiva* in Spanish). The Spanish sculptor Mariano Benlliure, however, misunderstood the commission, and instead depicted a 'native llama' (*llama nativa*) perched above her head! Thanks to this linguistic misunderstanding, a miniature camelid now takes its place on a statue in central Lima, providing photo opportunities for modern tourists. Together with military heroes and Inca princesses, llamas had become emblems of the new Andean nations, representing both a prime economic resource and a link to the pre-Hispanic past.

5 From the Andes to the Outback

In 1811 the first alpaca to be exhibited in Britain was put on show at Edward Cross's menagerie in London. The animal, which had been a pet in its native Lima, was 'remarkably tame' and had 'perforations in its ears in which ornamental rings had been placed'. It soon proved a great favourite with the British public, who admired its 'graceful attitudes, gentle disposition and playful manners' and expressed particular interest in its wool, which was thick, glossy and 'about eighteen inches long'. One admirer, Lady Liverpool, was

> so much . . . delighted with [the alpaca's] beauty, the softness and brilliancy of its coat and its animated and beaming features that she kissed it as if it had been a child, and had it turned loose on her lawn, in order that she might witness its movements free from restraint.[1]

The arrival of the alpaca in the aftermath of Spanish American independence led some Britons to think about acclimatization. Over the next four decades these ideas gained traction as increasing numbers of *lamas* were imported into Europe. Several treatises were published on the subject of alpaca acclimatization, some advising their naturalization in Scotland and Ireland, others suggesting their introduction to the colonies, particularly in

Australia. A daring operation to smuggle llamas and alpacas out of Peru was conducted in 1858 by Charles Ledger, who succeeded in transporting 256 of the animals to New South Wales. Camelid acclimatization formed part of a wider imperial project to appropriate and 'improve' exotic plants and animals, removing them from their native lands and cultivating them in suitable regions of the British Empire.[2]

Lamas first appeared in Britain in the 1800s and 1810s, during the Spanish American Wars of Independence. The first llama was exhibited at Brookes's Menagerie in London in 1805.[3] The animal owned by Edward Cross was shown in a private apartment in Piccadilly, alongside a male llama. Another alpaca featured in Ducrow's circus, where it was 'taught to gambol, kneel and lay down at the word of command'.[4] Llamas and alpacas appeared in zoological gardens by the 1820s and visited provincial towns in travelling menageries.[5] In 1814 the *Ipswich*

'Alpaca', designed and engraved by William Daniell, aquatint, 1812.

Journal reported that 'a new and beautiful race of animals from the snowy mountains of South America, called the Royal Alpaca and Llama' had recently been shown at Norwich and Yarmouth fairs.[6]

While living *lamas* initially functioned as sources of entertainment, alpaca wool was making important inroads into British commerce. Highly prized for its quality and softness, alpaca was used to make a variety of garments, mostly fashionable, high-end products. Dresses, shawls and umbrellas were all made from alpaca, as were coat linings, cravats and the occasional Scottish tartan.[7] Alpaca clothing was also valued in 'tropical climates' such as India, Jamaica and Africa, where British expatriates were 'thankful to possess a black coat which, while it has the appearance of broad cloth, is not a fourth of its weight'.[8] Sourced from Indian communities in the southern highlands of Peru, alpaca wool was purchased by itinerant British merchants and shipped to Liverpool and (to a much lesser extent) London. Bradford, already a key player in the woollen trade, became Britain's primary site for the manufacture of alpaca yarn and textiles, producing ever-increasing quantities of the material from the mid-1830s onwards.

Though alpaca wool was originally imported from Peru, plans arose in the 1840s to introduce the alpaca into Britain and thereby gain direct control over the trade. Advocates of the scheme anticipated multiple benefits. First, the naturalization of the alpaca would ensure a sufficient and continuous quantity of its wool, at a time when demand was outstripping supply. Second, the project would permit British farmers to make better use of their land, since alpacas would be able to survive in inhospitable mountain terrain unsuitable for cattle or sheep (some 30 million acres of which were believed to exist in the United Kingdom). Third, alpacas could be easily looked after,

'Walking Dress
in Red Alpaca',
*Illustrated London
News,* 28 August
1897.

their thick coats keeping them warm in the harshest winter and making it unnecessary 'to smear [them] with tar and butter as the farmers are obliged to do with the flocks in Scotland'. Fourth, the introduction of the alpaca would provide employment for impoverished labourers and artisans, and fifth, the alpaca might fulfil other economic functions, its meat forming 'an excellent ingredient for a pie' and its 'strong and pliant' skin offering a suitable material for bookbinding. The naturalization of the alpaca was presented as an important boost to the British textiles industry, a boon to agriculture and an antidote to various social problems. Enthusiasts identified the Scottish Highlands,

Thomas Weaver, *Llamas and a Fox in a Wooded Landscape*, 1828, oil on canvas.

Shetland, Wales, the Cheviot Hills, Dartmoor and the mountains of Kerry and Wicklow as the most promising regions for alpaca introduction, the terrain and climate of these locations most closely resembling those of the Andes.[9]

During the early 1840s, these ideas began to gain momentum, receiving increasing publicity and attracting the attention of some important local and national institutions. In 1840 the Tenth Annual Meeting of the British Association for the Advancement of Science featured a lecture by William Danson on the alpaca, during which samples of the wool and 'living specimens' of the animal were exhibited. In 1841 William Walton published an important article on the subject in the *Polytechnic Journal*, which he later extended into a short book, and in 1844 the Highland and Agricultural Society awarded 'a premium of Five Sovereigns and an honorary silver medal' to A. Gartshore Stirling of Craigbarnet for 'the best pair [of alpacas] born in the kingdom'. By the mid-1840s a number of improving landowners were rearing alpacas on their estates, some from mere curiosity but others with the intention of establishing a new line of business. Thomas Stevenson of Oban received several shipments of alpacas from his son

The Earl of Derby owned a flock of several alpacas and llamas at his estate in Cheshire. These were sold at auction on his death in 1851, along with the rest of his menagerie. 'Alpacas in the Knowsley Menagerie', *Illustrated London News*, 27 September 1851.

Alfred de Dreux, *Portrait of Queen Victoria and HRH Prince Albert on horseback, viewing the llamas in Windsor Great Park,* 1840s, oil on slate.

in Peru. Joseph Hegan Charles Tayleure and the Earl of Derby farmed small flocks of alpacas in Cheshire, while Robert Bell of Listowel, Kerry, introduced alpacas to Ireland. The queen's consort, Prince Albert, was another high-profile alpaca fancier, keeping several of the animals on the royal estate at Windsor.[10]

While the early signs were promising, the actual results of alpaca acclimatization were rather mixed. On the positive side, many owners did report success in keeping their animals alive, raising hopes that British alpacas, with superior care and nourishment, would produce a better grade of wool than that imported from Peru. Menagerist Edward Cross claimed that 'he noticed a visible improvement in the fleece of his alpaca, which he had shorn more than once, although the animal was kept under restraint and subjected to an unsuitable regimen, besides breathing the impure air of a populous town'.[11] Robert Bell contended, similarly, that the wool of his Irish alpacas was 'very much finer

112

than any alpaca wool I have yet seen imported into England'.[12] This prompted William Walton to suggest that careful British husbandry would facilitate an improvement of the species, the 'dirty and scurfy state' of imported wool being due to 'the deciduous habits of the Indian', who allowed his animals to become diseased 'through the want of seasonable shearing and the timely application of salve'.[13] Such ideas were very much in keeping with contemporary livestock rearing practices, which sought to raise the quality of animals through selective breeding and diet.[14]

Despite such upbeat testimonies, however, the overall picture was much less rosy, and a large number of alpacas succumbed to mismanagement and accident. Thomas Stevenson reported that of the dozen alpacas shipped to him by his son, only two, a male and a female, survived, despite an agreement made with the ship's captain that 'he was to receive a payment of freight one half of whatever number might arrive safe in England'. Another flock owned by Charles Tayleure was administered 'too strong medicine' by a shepherd, killing 'the greater part of them', while one of Bell's alpacas perished from eating a poisonous weed. Most disastrously, what should have been the largest single importation of alpacas into Britain ended in tragedy in 1842 when the captain of the *Sir Charles Napier* injudiciously stowed 274 of the animals above a cargo of guano (bird excrement), the 'effluvia' from the manure suffocating all but four of them.[15] Such setbacks highlighted the practical difficulties of animal acclimatization and pointed to the need for careful supervision and local knowledge. They did not, however, extinguish the hope that, with better planning and faster transportation, alpacas might be successfully introduced to the moors and highlands.

While early efforts to acclimatize the alpaca focused on Britain, in the 1850s attention shifted to British territories overseas. This was in part a response to the limited success of programmes such as Walton's to rear the alpaca in Britain itself. It also reflected the growing importance of the colonies in this period, and an increasing desire to ensure their economic viability. Both Cape Colony and the Indian province of Sindh were contemplated as suitable sites for the experiment, but it was in Australia that the project came to fruition. Two individuals played a key role in bringing this about: Edward Wilson and Charles Ledger.

Edward Wilson was a native of Victoria and editor of the *Melbourne Argus*. Together with a fellow colonist, Thomas Embling, Wilson promoted the introduction of new and useful animals to Australia, including camels, salmon and songbirds. The journalist quickly identified the alpaca as a promising candidate for naturalization and presented papers on the animal at the Philosophical Institute of Victoria. He expatiated at length on the potential benefits of alpaca acclimatization in the pages of the *Argus*, lobbying the colonial government for financial support.[16]

Early attempts to import alpacas directly to Victoria proved abortive, partly because of local scepticism, and partly because the Peruvian government's export ban made obtaining the animals difficult. In July 1858, however, when Wilson, then resident in London, heard that a flock of alpacas was up for auction in the British capital, he organized a campaign to raise funds for their purchase, requesting donations from fellow expatriate Australians and British manufacturers and using the letters pages of *The Times* to publicize his cause. By November sufficient money had been collected to buy ten of the alpacas and send them to Melbourne, where they were temporarily housed in the city's Botanical Gardens. The Bradford industrialist Titus Salt donated a further two alpacas from his private flock, raising the total number of animals to twelve, and providing two pure-bred males for breeding purposes. In 1863 a Birmingham gentleman, Alexander

James Duffield, set sail for Melbourne with a further 1,500 alpacas, collected in Bolivia with a special dispensation from the government.[17]

At the same time as Wilson was sourcing alpacas from Britain, another budding entrepreneur, Charles Ledger, was nearing the end of a decade-long project to introduce the species into New South Wales. A British merchant based in Tacna, Peru, Ledger had become interested in the alpaca business while employed by the firm Naylor's, who entrusted him with 'the purchase of alpaca and sheep's wool'. His job consisted of 'receiving from the Indians the different lots as they arrived from the interior . . . sorting the qualities and colours previous to packing . . . and finally shipping them, principally for account of Messrs. Christopher and James Rawdon, of Liverpool'.[18] Knowing how popular alpaca wool was in Europe, Ledger conceived the idea of introducing the Peruvian animal to Britain or one of its colonies and visited Sydney in 1852 to assess the feasibility of the scheme. The trip convinced him that 'the country was most admirably adapted for the alpaca', and he proceeded to assemble a large flock of alpacas and llamas at his estate at Chulluncayani near Peru's southern border, smuggling the animals across the Andes into the Argentine Confederation to circumvent the Peruvian government's camelid export ban. After several months in Laguna Blanca, accustoming the animals to their shipboard 'rations of dry alfalfa', Ledger re-crossed the Andes in perilous conditions and shipped them to Australia from the Chilean port of Caldera. Of the 322 animals stowed aboard the *Salvadora* in July 1858, 256 survived the voyage, arriving in Sydney four months later.[19]

The story of Ledger's quest to naturalize the alpaca reads like a classic Victorian adventure, replete with heroism, tragedy and adversity. At one point, two hundred of his flock perished from drinking the water of a lake 'infested with leeches'.[20] On another occasion he lost half his animals in a violent storm in the Andes; on a third two hundred alpacas died due to 'the negligence of one of the Indians'.[21] As well as enduring 'the hardships, personal danger and exhaustion suffered from cold, fatigue and privation' in the sierra, Ledger was repeatedly hounded by the Peruvian and Bolivian authorities who arrested him on two occasions and threatened to destroy his flock. With the courage and guile typical of the plucky Victorian entrepreneur, he managed, on both occasions, to outwit his captors, the first time by 'exercising his medical skills in the cure of the wife of the detaining prefect' and the second by slipping a dose of laudanum into his gaoler's 'grog'.[22] The setbacks, however, cost him seven years of his life and the entirety of his £7,000 fortune and though he ultimately succeeded in bringing alpacas to Australia he never fully recouped the money he had spent on the venture. Indeed, the farmers who had six years earlier expressed interest in Ledger's scheme were now cautious about the experiment, declining to buy the alpacas at auction. The colonial government was forced to step in and purchase the animals, arranging pasture for them at Sophienburg,

Charles Ledger crossed the Andes into Chile in March and April 1858. The journey was extremely gruelling and claimed the lives of 198 alpacas in just twenty days. Eighteen mules, 27 donkeys and 34 pack llamas also perished. 'Passage of Cordillera into Chile', *Annotated watercolour sketches by Santiago Savage, 1857–1858, being a record of Charles Ledger's journeys in Peru and Chile.*

Arthursleigh and Wingello and paying Ledger an annual salary of £1,300 to superintend their continued care.[23] Ledger thus benefited little from the introduction of the alpaca to Australia and, despite early successes in cross-breeding his animals, soon found their numbers declining. By 1865 most of the original alpacas had died, and their progeny were suffering from a form of mange, leading the colonial government to terminate its funding of the project and auction off the alpacas to the highest bidders.[24] As in Britain, alpaca acclimatization had fallen short of initial expectations, an outcome blamed, by turns, on inappropriate terrain, a severe drought in 1862–3, breeding from the females at too young an age and excessive (or, according to some, insufficient) government interference.[25] It was a similar story in Victoria, where all of Wilson's original alpacas were dead and the only survivor of Duffield's 1,500-strong flock was 'a solitary white lamb – a very pretty and lively specimen of alpaca juvenility'.[26]

The alpaca naturalization scheme clearly reflects the social and spatial dimensions of nineteenth-century science and illustrates some of the diplomatic, commercial and scholarly networks that connected Britain and Latin America. Though not part of Britain's formal empire, the newly independent states of South America were closely integrated into British trade routes and were soon staffed with a regiment of British consular officials, many of whom furthered the study of natural history by shipping native plants and animals to British institutions.[27] Former soldiers who had gone to Spanish America to fight in the wars of independence often remained in the region for some time, while British merchants travelled to the continent to sell manufactures and purchase raw materials, establishing important connections with local people and sometimes marrying into creole families.[28] A host of naturalists also descended on South America in the years after independence, some taking up positions at local museums and universities, others conducting research on behalf of scientific institutions back in Europe. Individuals from all of these backgrounds played a role in the alpaca naturalization project, offering up their zoological, social and technological expertise on both sides of the Atlantic (and indeed Pacific).

First, alpaca importers relied heavily on the knowledge and experience of indigenous Peruvians, whose long contact with the animals made them experts on their needs and behaviour. Though Native Americans were often accused of failing to exploit the full potential of the alpaca and of duping gullible foreigners into buying old or diseased beasts, their expertise in farming alpacas was grudgingly acknowledged. William Walton advocated enlisting Peruvian keepers to bring alpacas to Britain on the grounds that they knew best how to handle them – and would themselves be 'improved' by absorption into British culture.

I should . . . advise that each shipment, if large, be accompanied by a Peruvian llanero, or shepherd, one accustomed to manage these animals, acquainted with their tempers and experienced in the cure of their diseases. Young men of this class might easily be had at a trifling expense; and, if Indians, a little tuition and intercourse with Europeans would change their disposition and induce them to improve their habits.[29]

Charles Ledger likewise relied on the expertise of Native Americans, hiring twelve Bolivian shepherds to care for his flock en route to Australia. The men remained with the alpacas until 1860, and were assigned the task of shearing the Australian flock in 1859 due to their intimate connection with the animals. As the *Sydney Morning Herald* explained,

It was thought desirable that these men, though rather clumsy manipulators, should do the work in preference to regular [sheep] shearers, as their long familiarity with the animals has imparted to them a degree of docility and quietness while in the hands of their own keepers which they would not preserve in the presence of strangers.[30]

Native Peruvians thus proved essential to alpaca relocation, though their knowledge was not always freely given or treated with respect. Ledger, for example, complained that his indigenous helpers would not shear pregnant females alpacas, on the grounds that 'they would miscarry and die were [they] to shear them' – a view he attributed to superstition.[31]

If Native American expertise helped with the day to day management of the alpacas, the collaboration of sailors in the British navy and merchant marine also proved critical in their successful relocation. This was recognized by proponents of acclimatization, who offered detailed advice on how and where to ship alpacas with the most profitable results. Walton, for instance, conscious that a shorter crossing would improve the odds of keeping the alpacas alive, advised transporting the animals to Panama on a new line about to be set up by the Pacific Steam Navigation Company, allowing them to recuperate on the Isthmus for six weeks and then shipping them to England from the Caribbean port of Chagre.[32] Another alpaca enthusiast, in this case from Tasmania, suggested that 'it might be possible for some of the vessels trading to San Francisco to procure a few [alpacas], by means of vessels from Chili [sic], there being a considerable communication between San Francisco and Valparaíso'.[33] The extension of British shipping to the Pacific in the wake of Spanish American independence and the increasing sophistication of steam-powered vessels in the mid-nineteenth century cut down journey times across the world's oceans, making it more likely that animals would survive the crossing to distant lands. Some sailors also went the extra mile to look after their live cargo, further improving survival rates. In 1841, for example, Captain Bottomley of the *Highlander* took great care to convey nine alpacas from Valparaíso to Liverpool, feeding them on a diet of lucern and even 'washing the mouths of the animals before eating and drinking' to keep them healthy.[34]

While indigenous people and British mariners thus played an important role in caring for transient alpacas, the impetus behind the acclimatization schemes came largely from British subjects based in Spanish America. Commercial links were particularly important. Charles Ledger, as we have seen, was introduced to the alpaca through his job as a wool merchant, working first as a clerk for the house of Naylor's and later operating his own business. The Briton further ensconced himself in Peruvian society by 'marrying into an influential family in Tacna', forging important connections with the local community.[35]

The contribution of another alpaca advocate, General John O'Brien, illustrates even more clearly the role of itinerant Britons in appropriating the alpaca. An Irishman by birth, from Baltinglass, County Wicklow, O'Brien travelled to South America in 1812 to open a merchant house in Buenos Aires, but ended up fighting in the Spanish American Wars of Independence as General José de San Martín's aide-de-camp. After the conflict concluded, O'Brien settled in Peru and engaged in mining ventures. On returning to Britain he became increasingly enthusiastic about the prospect of naturalizing the alpaca in his native Ireland and wrote a series of letters to his old Peruvian friends, urging them to cooperate with William Danson's naturalization scheme. One of O'Brien's correspondents, Peter Murphy, HM Consul at Arica, was entreated to offer his 'aid and assistance' to 'whatever person [Danson] may send out to this country' to collect alpacas, with a view to conferring 'a national gift' upon 'your dear old mountains of Wicklow'. Another, Michael Crawley, Prefect of the department of Lampa, was requested, for the sake of 'old friendship', to help with selecting good-quality alpacas and 'conducting them to the coast'. The content of these letters, with its emphasis on friendship and service to one's country, highlights the value of personal contacts in furthering scientific and economic plans.[36]

Back in Britain, the successful rearing and exploitation of the alpaca depended on input from three other communities of 'experts': men of science, engineers and zoo professionals. The first of these, men of science, conducted observations on alpacas and studied their anatomy and physiology. The famous comparative anatomist Richard Owen delivered a lecture on the 'peculiar properties' of alpaca wool at the Society of Arts in 1851, in which he noted its 'glossy . . . silky' quality.[37] Another scientist, Alfred Higginson of the Natural History Society of Liverpool, dissected two alpacas, observing that 'the water cells' in their stomachs 'were either empty or partly filled with masticated food in a semi-fluid state'.[38] Anatomical findings helped acclimatizers to better understand the needs of the animal and the climatic conditions in which they might thrive.

While zoologists debated the pros and cons of transporting and farming the alpaca, the use of alpaca wool for textile production was made possible by a series of technological developments, most of them the work of enterprising Yorkshire artisans. Since it was finer and longer than sheep's wool, the fleece of the alpaca could not be spun using traditional machinery, but required specially adapted spinning apparatus. Initially, no such apparatus was available. In the 1830s, however, Benjamin Outram, 'a scientific manufacturer of Gretland near Halifax', designed a machine that could spin alpaca wool economically and effectively, giving rise to a new industry.[39] Titus Salt installed Outram's machinery in his worsted factories in Bradford in 1836, and was soon producing alpaca goods on an industrial scale. The technical expertise of British artisans, who had perhaps never seen a living alpaca, thus played a crucial role in stimulating the demand for their wool, and, in time, the desire for their naturalization.

Finally, in highlighting the communities that facilitated alpaca introduction, we ought to mention one last group: zookeepers. When seeking advice on alpaca acclimatization, alpaca advocates frequently invoked the practical knowledge of these individuals, whose direct experience of rearing alpacas in Britain made them the next best thing to Peruvian Indians when it came to learning about the animals' diet and habits. Danson, for instance, collaborated with Thomas Atkins of Liverpool Zoological Gardens, compiling a circular to be issued to ships' captains 'for their guide in treatment of the animals during the voyage'.[40] Walton, meanwhile, quizzed Edward Cross, director of the menagerie at Exeter 'Change, about the alpaca, citing the

Llamas and alpacas featured in both scientific journals and popular natural histories. This image comes from a popular magazine, *The Museum of Animated Nature* (1848).

547.—Vicugna.

548.—Guanaco.

549.—Male Brown Wild Llama or Guanaco.

550.—Paco.

551.—Guanaco and Tame White Llama.

552.—Guanaco.

551.—Foot of Llama.

554.—White Llama.

Pictorial Museum

[THE MUSEUM OF ANIMATED NATURE.]

THE ALPACAS.
In the Garden of the Zoological Society

Zoological Society of London: two alpacas standing in a mountainous landscape. Coloured etching by A. A. Park after W. Panormo, 1829.

latter's testimony that the animal in his possession subsisted on 'dry food, such as hay, beans and oats', that 'it never drank anything the whole time I had it' and that he cured it of a skin complaint (the 'itch') by 'rubbing a little mercurial ointment on the spine'.[41] Though Cross was a showman, and not a professional naturalist, Walton seems to have valued his opinions highly and was happy to rely on his expertise: 'Few men', he remarked, 'could be found more intelligent or more observant than Mr Cross.'[42]

Even travelling menageries, usually perceived as mere sources of entertainment, could assist the alpaca acclimatization project.

When showmistress Mrs Wombwell exhibited a 'jet black' alpaca in Liverpool in 1853, the animal attracted considerable attention from local farmers, generating a series of letters to the *Liverpool Mercury*. The *Mercury* initiated the conversation, observing that the animal was 'entitled to much attention, not merely from motives of curiosity, but from the immense mercantile advantages which would accrue to the agriculturalist as well as the manufacturer by its naturalisation in this country'. In the following weeks, letters appeared from readers concurring with this view. One correspondent, 'G. G.', who had seen the menagerie specimen, noted that the alpaca's fleece typically weighed 'from 12 to 14 lbs [5.4 to 6.4 kg]', though 'on the one before us at Wombwell's (which, however, is singularly fine), we should imagine upwards of 20 lbs [9 kg]'. He went on to express his hope that the *Mercury*'s article would 'induce the owners or holders of hilly or mountainous districts at once to consider' the 'practicability' of domesticating the alpaca there. A second correspondent, 'T. F.', broadly agreed with these sentiments, requesting information on 'where the breed may be obtained at a price commensurate with the great risk which must be run before any return can be expected', and where he might find an 'able treatise' explaining how to avoid 'accidents arising from ignorance of the habits of the animal'.[43] While sailors, merchants and naturalists thus brought the first alpacas back to British shores, it was often travelling entertainers who introduced them to people in the provinces, and who, through long experience, understood best how to manage them.

If alpaca naturalization illustrated the complex networks of exchange and expertise at work within and beyond the British Empire, it also exposed certain tensions in these relationships. Alpacas, it turned out, meant different things to different people.

The British, the Australians and, as we shall see, the French all invested these valuable animals with their own specific hopes and expectations. Even within Britain and its Antipodean possessions there were varying regional and local interests at stake. These different aspirations were not necessarily mutually exclusive; what was good for farmers in New South Wales might also be beneficial to textile workers in Bradford. They do, nonetheless, betray different priorities and emphases. As in the Spanish Empire, camelids quickly became linked to national and regional prosperity.

Firstly, viewed from a British perspective, alpacas were intended to promote the nation's commerce and revitalize its agriculture by transforming barren and uncultivated regions into useful pastures. Their introduction would permit more effective use of Britain's farmland, already exploited as far as possible by native species, and would enable the British to produce a fine and delicate fabric capable of competing with the best French silks. It would also reduce Britain's dependence on Peruvian wool imports, which contemporaries considered unreliable, expensive and insufficient to meet demand. To this extent, the acclimatization project was a tangible reflection of Britain's naval dominance and imperial reach, a demonstration of its technological and agricultural expertise and a testament to its commercial penetration of post-independence South America. By the same token, however, the desire to naturalize the alpaca was also an expression of British anxieties and economic vulnerability, at a time when manufacturers were worrying about foreign competition (Germany and the USA were beginning to industrialize) and the prospect of civil war in the USA threatened cotton supplies.[44] Britons feared that if they did not acclimatize the alpaca, European rivals would take the initiative, threatening the country's dominance in the woollen trade and putting manufacturers out of work. Alpaca naturalization was thus perceived as an antidote

'Sketches in the International Exhibition', *Illustrated London News*, 9 September 1871.

to actual and potential national problems, as well as a marker of imperial dominance.

While alpaca acclimatization was intended to benefit Britain as a whole, specific regions and cities took particular interest in the project, developing their own local connections with the alpaca. The Irishman General O'Brien, for example, though happy to collaborate with British colleagues in bringing alpacas to the British Isles, was particularly interested in the benefits the scheme would confer upon his home county of Wicklow, where he thought alpacas would do well.[45] Similar sentiments were at work in Liverpool, where William Danson and zoo director Thomas Atkins seem to have perceived alpaca importation as a source of local pride for one of Britain's main trading hubs with South America, and another way of advertising the port city's

global reach and entrepreneurial spirit. In Bradford, meanwhile,
the alpaca was regarded as essential to the city's textile prosperity,
earning the West Yorkshire town royal patronage in 1845 after
local artisans converted the fleece of one of Prince Albert's alpacas
into an apron and 'a striped and figured dress'. In April of that
year a public dinner was held at the Bradford Exchange Rooms at
which 'a painted representation of the Alpaca' was displayed
alongside Bradford's coat of arms. In 1851, when Salt constructed
a special village for his employees, alpaca emblems were chiselled
into several of the buildings, and by 1859 Bradford even boasted
an 'Alpaca Beer-house' – further testimony of the animal's local
significance and its incorporation into popular culture.[46] These
cases suggest that there was a regional as well as a national dimension to alpaca naturalization as different counties and cities
sought specific benefits as farmers, importers and manufacturers
of alpaca produce.

Alpaca emblem on Saltaire cricket club badge.

Shifting our focus to Australia, we find a further difference in emphasis, though also an awareness of the wider imperial and local circumstances noted above. On the one hand, rearing the animals in the Outback was considered good for the British Empire as a whole and beneficial in particular to textile-producing cities like Bradford. On the other hand, the Australian alpaca programme had a specifically colonial dimension, and was deeply inflected with elements of local pride – sometimes broadly 'Australian', but in other instances confined more narrowly to a single Australian state. Seeking contributions to his alpaca fund in *The Times*, Wilson expressed his hope that 'Australians now in England' would supply the money to buy the animals and recommended that the flock be sent to 'Victoria, if possible', thus benefiting his native Melbourne.[47] Commenting on Ledger's achievements, meanwhile, the British newspaper *The Era* concluded that 'if there is a man who has *done well* for

Australia it is Charles Ledger, and we trust the colony will mark
its sense of his merit in a manner befitting a government to
bestow, and a public benefactor to receive'.[48] Colonial and
imperial pride were thus at stake in the alpaca exchange project,
as British papers admonished Australian subjects to show due
gratitude towards a metropolitan benefactor and the inhabitants
of rival settlements competed for regional pride and economic
advantage – all within the wider context of the British Empire.
At the 1862 International Exhibition the government of New
South Wales received a medal for 'the first alpaca wool grown in
the colony' and Ledger 'obtained honourable mention for excel-
lence of quality of alpaca tallow and pomade' – a source of pride
for the nascent colony.[49]

Finally, looking beyond the British Empire, we find a similar
desire to naturalize the alpaca in other European countries, several of which also associated camelids with national and regional
prosperity. In Holland, for instance, King William II installed a
flock of thirty alpacas in a royal park near The Hague.[50] In Spain,

meanwhile, Mariano de la Paz Graells reared a mixed flock of llamas and alpacas at Aranjuez, hoping to improve their wool through selective breeding.[51] Most active of all were the French, who established a Jardin d'Acclimatation in the Bois de Boulogne in 1860 and experimented with interbreeding the different camelids, producing 'crosses between the llama, the alpaca and the guanaco'.[52] In 1851, M. E. Deville published a short tract recommending the rearing of the animal in the mountains of the Pyrenees, the Alps, the Vosges, the Auvergne and France's newly acquired colony, Algeria. Several years later, the Société Imperiale Zoologique d'Acclimatation awarded a prize of 2,000 francs to Eugene Roehn for 'the introduction in the mountains of Europe or Algeria of a flock of pure-bred alpacas'.[53] As in Britain, particular regions forged strong links with the alpaca, in this case the area around Nancy, Lorraine, where the local acclimatization society focused most of its efforts on llama naturalization and succeeded in breeding the animals in the Vosges before the entire flock succumbed to a skin disease in 1864 (probably scabies).[54] In France, too, alpaca acclimatization was billed as a benefit to the nation's economy, a boon to individual regions and a springboard for colonial prosperity.

By the end of the nineteenth century, therefore, the alpaca and the llama had spread across the globe. Once confined to the Peruvian Andes, alpacas and llamas were now to be found in the mountains of Scotland, the lowlands of the Netherlands, the parched interior of New South Wales and even the streets of New York. Alpaca wool was rolling off the production lines in the form of jackets, waistcoats and umbrellas, while alpaca acclimatization was touted as a major agricultural innovation and a source of substantial profits. With the latest techniques in animal husbandry, European farmers and their colonial colleagues hoped to improve both the quality and quantity of the animals' wool,

providing a more reliable source of yarn for manufacturers. The Acclimatisation Society of Melbourne, for instance, alleged that 'the South American Indian' had failed to maximize the alpaca's potential, but predicted great improvements in the species now that the animal was 'subjected for the first time to the same treatment that has effected such wonders with the Leicester, Lincoln or South Down sheep, the short-horn ox [and] the thorough-bred horse'.[55]

In reality, of course, acclimatization proved much harder than its supporters had anticipated. Animals died when transplanted to unfamiliar climates. Farmers got cold feet about experimenting with new stock. Disease wreaked havoc within small camelid populations and wars and revolutions thwarted naturalization projects. In Britain, alpacas were sold regularly by animal traders like the Liverpool dealer William Cross, but never in large enough numbers to establish a serious breeding programme.[56] In Australia, Ledger's flock ended up depleted and scattered, while in New Zealand, a solitary alpaca was exhibited at the Fielding Show in 1909 'merely as a curiosity', the sole survivor of a flock of 21 imported to the country by Mr R. Rhodes some years earlier.[57] A dejected Ledger returned to Peru in 1865 'without one shilling to my name, having lost all I had in the realization of an enterprise I fondly hoped would have conferred great benefits on a thriving colony of my own country'.[58] Despite these setbacks, however, the nineteenth-century acclimatization schemes opened the way for later successful naturalization efforts, putting camelids on the radar of British merchants in Arequipa, textile magnates in Bradford and sheep farmers in New South Wales.

6 A Very Modern Llama

Nineteenth-century acclimatization efforts may have been unsuccessful, but the twentieth and twenty-first centuries have witnessed the emergence of the llama as a global animal. Llamas and alpacas have been successfully introduced into Europe, North America and Australasia, where they are farmed for their wool and meat and kept as pets. In Peru and Bolivia, meanwhile, camelids remain important cultural referents, providing a valuable export and playing a very visible role in the growing tourist industry. Whether posing for tourists in Cusco, guarding sheep in the Swiss Alps or attending weddings in Japan, llamas continue to make their mark on the modern world.

In Peru, alpaca wool remains pivotal to the economy and constitutes one of the country's key exports. Of the 3.5 million alpacas thought to live in the world today, three million live in Peru, with a further 500,000 in Bolivia, the second largest producer of alpaca fibre. According to the International Alpaca Association, Peru exports an average of 4,000 tons of alpaca fibre every year, mostly to China, Italy and the United Kingdom. It also exports a range of finished alpaca goods, predominantly to the United States. In 2002 the Peruvian Centre for Social Studies calculated that some 65,000 rural families in Peru were dependent on alpaca farming to make a living, highlighting the continued centrality of the animal to the nation's economy.[1]

Two girls pose for tourist photographs with fluffy white alpacas, La Raya, Peru.

The vast majority of Peruvian alpaca wool is produced by small-scale farmers from indigenous communities in the sierra. The Puno region is the prime location for alpaca farming, followed by the neighbouring states of Cusco and Arequipa. In 2013 the Province of Caylloma, near Arequipa, had '3,500 families involved in farming some 400,000 alpacas and 50,000 llamas', producing 6,500 kg of fibre and 36,000 kg of meat each year.[2] To sell their wool, small-scale herders typically travel to regional fairs, where alpaca fibre is purchased by middlemen, known as *alcanzadores* (pursuers). The *alcanzadores* then re-sell the wool to *rescatistas* (agents), who buy on behalf of one of the large fibre producers located in Arequipa. Here the wool is sorted according to colour and quality and sent for processing, with fine, white wool commanding the highest prices. Though there are around five hundred different companies engaged in the export of alpaca wool, fifteen major manufacturers dominate the market, enjoying foreign investment and technological backing denied to their smaller, family-run competitors. Today, Michell and Grupo Inca are among the most important exporters of Peruvian alpaca fibre.

The four stages of alpaca wool production:

1) Alpacas grazing in a corral high in the Andes.

2) Sorting alpaca wool for length, colour and quality.

3) Dyeing and spinning the wool.

As well as providing wool for the world market, llamas and alpacas provide subsistence for many Andean families, who make clothes from their wool and consume the meat of dead animals. Alpaca meat is considered a delicacy in Peru, and forms an important source of protein for peasant communities, along with guinea pig. Llamas also continue to feature in Andean rituals, reflecting the persistence of pre-conquest belief systems. In Cusco, two festivals are held every August to pay homage to the llama. In one, Llama's T'inkay, llamas are adorned with

4) Selling luxury alpaca products.

colourful earrings called tulunpi, believed to stimulate herd fertility; in another, Llama's Ch'allay, chicha (a maize-based alcoholic drink) is poured over the animals' bodies as thanks for their provision of wool and meat.[3] Llamas and alpacas are sacrificed in the *wilancho*, a ceremony that accompanies the building of houses, while in Bolivia llama foetuses called *sullus* are buried under houses for good luck. When an alpaca is killed by lightning, another is sacrificed to placate the spirits, supposedly preventing further animals from dying.[4]

The government of Peru is very conscious of the value of alpaca wool to the country's economy and has instituted breeding

Llama foetuses on sale at the Witches' Market in La Paz, 2015.

programmes to improve the quality of the fibre. In 1984 the International Alpaca Association was founded in Arequipa to 'protect the image of the alpaca fiber and its derivatives, as well as [to promote the] international consumption and ensure the quality of their products'.[5] In 2003, meanwhile, the Peruvian government promulgated Law No. 28041 to promote 'the rearing, production, commercialization and consumption of domestic South American camelids', establishing genealogical registers for both llamas and alpacas so that the best examples of each could be bred and maintained.[6] These initiatives are intended to raise the value of wool exports and to counteract competition from foreign alpaca producers in countries like Australia, where alpacas can be farmed on a larger scale and their breeding more closely monitored (see below). Since 2012 Peru has even held an annual 'Alpaca Day', an event designed to increase awareness and consumption of alpaca products.[7]

While the national government has thus taken steps to nurture and improve the alpaca, more regional initiatives have also

had an impact, reflecting the vital importance of alpaca to particular areas of the country. In the southern region of Puno, where the highest number of alpaca farms are located, an ordinance was passed in June 2013 declaring the alpaca 'an animal . . . representative both typically and ancestrally of the region' and making it a priority to 'facilitate and promote the raising of the alpaca for the production of its fibre and the protection of its genetic biodiversity'.[8] With assistance from Oxfam, alpaca farmers in Puno have been able to improve the quality of their stock through a programme of genetic selection. In 2006 the Munay Paq'ocha ('beautiful alpaca') laboratory was founded in Macusani, 'the alpaca capital of the world', to test alpaca wool with the latest technology and identify the best animals for breeding.[9]

Across the border in Bolivia there has been a similar push to promote alpaca production. In 2006 the International Fund for Agricultural Development launched a project to support alpaca producers and improve the health of their animals. The project introduced new techniques to treat stomach parasites and other diseases common to camelids. It also established local co-operatives for spinning and weaving the wool and drying alpaca meat. These innovations have provided an essential boost to the local economy, increasing agricultural output in Latin America's poorest country.[10]

In November 2014, the Bolivian government began lobbying the United Nations to make 2016 the International Year of Camelids. The draft resolution submitted to the UN General Assembly emphasized the 'economic and cultural importance of camelids in the lives of people living in areas where they are domesticated' and stressed the need to 'raise awareness at all levels to promote the protection of camelids and the consumption of the goods produced from these mammals in a sustainable way'.[11] Though the resolution ultimately failed, its introduction

A baby llama frolics at Machu Picchu, Peru's most famous archaeological site.

This contemporary tapestry illustrates the centrality of camelids to Andean society. Alpacas graze in the foreground, a llama is about to be loaded with bags of potatoes in the centre and fluffy vicuñas inhabit the high *puna* in the background.

Learning about llamas at a school in the Peruvian *puna*. According to the text, the llama 'has a long neck, two ears, two eyes, a snout, four legs and a tail, and is coffee-coloured'.

is testimony to the importance of camelids to Bolivians. Llamas and alpacas thus continue to occupy a central role in the economies of Peru and Bolivia, shaping identity at both a national and a regional level.

The alpaca's wild relative the vicuña has had a more traumatic path into the twentieth century, though it now appears to be on the road to recovery. By the 1960s, overhunting had left the vicuña critically endangered and on the verge of extinction, with a mere 6,000 vicuñas in the wild in 1974. The Convention on International Trade in Endangered Species (CITES) recognized the animal's perilous status in 1975, placing the species on Appendix I and banning any form of trade in its fleece. Governments in Peru, Bolivia, Chile and Argentina issued legislation to protect vicuñas within their territories and signed an international agreement in 1979 (along with Ecuador) to co-ordinate conservation efforts. In 1967 the first of several special reserves for vicuñas was established in Pampa Galeras, Peru, where the animals could be monitored and protected.[12]

Thanks to these conservation measures, the decline in the vicuña population has been halted and their numbers have started to increase. By 2015 it was estimated that there were 340,000 vicuñas in the Andean highlands of Peru, Bolivia, Argentina and Chile, with the vast majority concentrated in Peru.[13] The species has been downgraded to Appendix II on CITES, and is now considered out of immediate danger. Classed as a Peruvian heritage species, the vicuña still cannot be hunted, but it can be shorn and released by indigenous people using the traditional Inca *chakku* technique. With vicuña numbers continuing to rise, there is cautious optimism about the animal's future and hope that its controlled exploitation may benefit impoverished local people.

There is, however, no room for complacency. Conservationists have expressed fears about the possible stress caused to vicuñas by catch and release shearing, which may impact on their health, fertility and physical well-being. Vicuñas that have been shorn

Vicuñas graze in the Salinas y Aguada Blanca National Reserve, Peru.

144

may be unable to cope with temperature extremes high in the Andes; human interference during the *chakku* may lead to the separation of *crias* from mothers; injuries may be sustained during shearing; shearing may cause stress to pregnant females resulting in a miscarriage; and muscle damage caused during the *chakku* may prevent the animals from escaping from predators (pumas and foxes) or impair their ability to find food or shelter.[14] Criticisms have also been made of recent attempts to subject vicuñas to captive-management (rearing the animals within fenced enclosures), which may cause changes in behaviour and increase the animals' vulnerability to disease.[15]

Most seriously, poaching continues to present problems, fuelled in part by the legalization of the wool trade. With trade in legally obtained vicuña wool permitted since 1997, it is harder to identify the origin of fleeces, and easier for poachers to smuggle illegal skins on to the market. This, coupled with a rise in demand for vicuña wool, has led to an increase in illegal hunting. In December 2013, for instance, hunters slaughtered 93 vicuñas in the region of Huancavelica and escaped with their fleeces.[16] The transition from conservation to sustainable use will need to be carefully managed if the vicuña is to survive in the long term.

Outside South America, the number of llamas and alpacas has grown substantially in the last twenty years. Until 1993, the export of camelids from Peru was banned, and the vast majority of animals were confined to zoological gardens. After the ban was lifted, however, mass exportation began, and alpacas – and to a lesser extent llamas – have emerged as popular hobby farm animals across the globe. Today, there are thought to be around 300,000 alpacas in the USA, 300,000 in Australia, 35,000 in the UK and 23,000 in New Zealand, though this remains only a fraction of the total world population.[17]

Peruvian political party Tierra y Libertad uses a vicuña on its logo. Tierra y Libertad is a left-wing party from the Cusco region which promotes 'indigenous rights' and 'the conservation and care of Mother Earth'.

While not as economically and socially important in the West as they are in South America, llamas and alpacas fulfil a variety of functions outside Peru, some of them familiar, others entirely novel. The majority of llamas and alpacas in the anglophone world are reared as pets, a cute and exotic addition to any live-stock holding. Others, however, have been put to use, providing services to a broader range of consumers.

First, as in South America, llamas have been employed as car-riers of people and goods. An article of 1 April 1912 in *The Times* noted that in 1911 London Zoo recruited a llama to pull 'small children' around the grounds in a pony cart and in 1912 it began using a white alpaca for the same purpose. In 1907, meanwhile, Mr A. W. Wingfield experimented with riding llamas at his pri-vate menagerie at Ampthill, Bedfordshire, prompting speculation that camelids might be used for fox hunting and even in war as a 'solution of the problem of the scarcity of horses'.[18] Today, llamas are used for trekking and occasionally as golf caddies!

'Inquisitive Llama'. Six-week-old Chesney poses for the camera at Chessington Zoo, Surrey, 1938.

Spotnik the baby llama, Lincoln Park Zoo, Chicago, 1958. The llama sports a 'sack dress' to 'keep the animal from biting a spot on its hide', though he appears 'to be checking to see if there's anything else to wear'.

'Let's try it on George'. Keepers at London Zoo vacuum clean a llama, 1938. George 'stands tense', 'ears alert'.

Princesses Elizabeth and Margaret ride in the llama cart at London Zoo, 1939.

'Some Quaint Mounts'. Riding llamas at A. W. Wingfield's menagerie in Bedfordshire. Wingfield also experimented with riding camels and ostriches. *The Bystander*, 7 August 1907.

An alpaca pasty, made from Cornish alpaca.

Since the 1990s alpacas have also begun to be raised intensively for their wool. Though most alpaca farms are small scale, some larger ranches have appeared in the USA and Australia. The Ambersun Alpacas business at Mount Compass, south of Adelaide, had more than 1,000 alpacas in 2013.

Though alpaca meat is little eaten in the West, attempts are being made to promote it, leading to its emergence as a high-end dish.[19] Alpaca flesh has the lowest cholesterol level of any meat – 0.16 per cent – making it an extremely healthy form of sustenance. In 2007 the Australian Alpaca Association published a brochure on the nutritional value of various cuts of alpaca meat, featuring recipes for alpaca sausage, alpaca soup and alpaca steak.[20]

Another, more recent, innovation is the 'guard llama'. Known for their acrid spit and vicious kicks, llamas and alpacas have been used in various parts of the globe to protect sheep, calves and poultry from predators. In Switzerland, where wolves have begun to re-colonize the Alps, llamas have been drafted in to defend the local sheep. In the American West, llamas are often employed to counter attacks from coyotes, while in 2008 a farm in Camborne, Cornwall, hired two alpacas, William and Harry, to protect free-range chickens from foxes.[21] Llamas can police around twenty to fifty sheep at a time and are cheaper to maintain than guard dogs.

Punch proposes using llamas for hunting, along with kangaroos, giraffes and rhinoceroses, 7 April 1909.

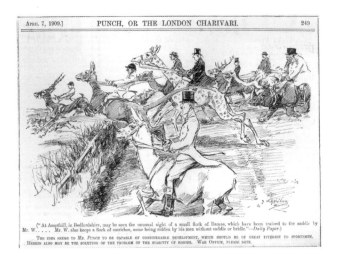

("At Ampthill, in Bedfordshire, may be seen the unusual sight of a small flock of llamas, which have been trained to the saddle by Mr. W.... Mr. W. also keeps a flock of ostriches, some being ridden by his men without saddle or bridle."—*Daily Paper*.)

THE IDEA SEEMS TO MR. *PUNCH* TO BE CAPABLE OF CONSIDERABLE DEVELOPMENT, WHICH SHOULD BE OF GREAT INTEREST TO SPORTSMEN. HEREIN ALSO MAY BE THE SOLUTION OF THE PROBLEM OF THE SCARCITY OF HORSES. WAR OFFICE, PLEASE NOTE.

When they spot a predator, they will sound the alarm, approach, spit on and kick the assailant, often causing it serious injury. Studies suggest that flock damage is radically reduced when llamas are on patrol.[22]

As well as protecting livestock, camelids have been used to help people. Animal-assisted therapy has become increasingly popular in recent years, with a growing recognition that interaction with other species can have a positive psychological effect on a range of mental, physical and emotional conditions.[23] Cats and dogs are the most common therapy animals, but llamas have also been enlisted for this purpose. A llama named Rojo conducts regular visits to hospitals, schools and old people's homes in Canada and the northwest USA, while his companion, an alpaca called Napoleon, was filmed kissing residents at a nursing home in Beaverton, Oregon. Some llama shows even include a special category called 'public relations', where a llama's aptitude for therapy is assessed through tasks such as lowering its head to greet someone in a wheelchair.[24] Environmental enrichment of this kind has been shown to de-stress patients and accelerate recovery from illness. A very early instance of llama therapy occurred in 1873 when Sydney breeder Thomas Holt donated alpacas to 'the lunatic asylums at Parramatta and the Cook's River' for the entertainment of inmates.[25]

Some camelid owners, of course, are more interested in their animals' appearance than their utility, and for these individuals, livestock shows offer the chance to exhibit pedigree animals for prizes. National and regional alpaca associations have been formed in the USA, Britain and Australia to establish breeding standards and competitions are held on a regular basis, with different classes based on colour, age and wool-type (huacaya or suri). Judges rank alpacas on the conformation of their bodies and the quality of their wool, which is assessed for fineness, lustre, crimp, uniformity, staple length and density. They also

A llama caddy stands by while golfers sink a putt, Sherwood Forest Golf Club, North Carolina, 2009.

inspect the animals' teeth and observe their gait when walking. According to the British Alpaca Association, 'between 300–4,000 registered animals are shown in organised events' in Britain every year.[26] While most competitions are serious events, others are predominantly for fun, offering classes for alpaca agility and fancy-dress opportunities. The 2009 Minnesota livestock fair featured a special costume round, with llamas dressed as giraffes, brides, clowns and even the Statue of Liberty.

In Japan, you can now have an alpaca at your wedding! A hotel in Tochigi, just north of Tokyo, offers a special wedding package where couples can walk down the aisle accompanied by a fluffy camelid wearing a snazzy bow tie. The animal stands by while the nuptials are completed and then joins the newly-weds for photographs once the ceremony is over. It is later returned to a nearby zoo. The novel experience costs around 50,000 yen (about $400 or £350) and is seen as a trendy modern take on the traditional Shinto wedding.[27]

Llama Daddy Warbucks entertains residents at the Spokane Rehabilitation Center, Washington, 1977.

In recent years, a few llamas have even become media phenomena. In November 2013 a llama named Serge hit the headlines when a group of drunken French students liberated him from a circus in Bordeaux and took him for a ride aboard a tram. Serge has since become a local celebrity, appearing as a mascot for the city's football team.[28] In February 2015 another llama drama captivated America when two llamas escaped in Sun City, Arizona, and went on the run. The chase was filmed by a local TV company and broadcast live across the USA. Thousands of people followed the coverage, filling social media with references to 'llamageddon' and 'Isllamaphobia' and nicknaming the animals Bonnie and Clyde to reflect their fugitive status. The llamas were eventually separated and captured with a lasso – a finale with echoes of the Wild West.[29] So llamas and alpacas have graced our screens and Twitter feeds as well as our fields.

If real llamas have provided sustenance, protection and entertainment, fictional llamas have made their mark in the cultural sphere. By turns elegant, iconic, cuddly and crotchety, llamas and alpacas have inspired a number of artistic and literary representations. They have featured in poems, novels and films and provided the subject matter for songs, advertisements and computer games.

Some of the most memorable portrayals of llamas have appeared in literature for children. These tend to focus on two key llama qualities: their propensity to spit and the fact that 'llama' rhymes with 'pyjama'. Hergé's *bande dessinée* album, *Tin Tin and the Temple of the Sun* (1949), for example, chronicles the young hero's travels to Peru, where a vengeful llama spits on his friend, Captain Haddock. Catherine Ipcizade's *'Twas the Day Before Zoo Day* (2007) features drooling llamas who 'won't quit spitting', while Diane Crane's *Stop Spitting at Your Brother* (1996) tells the story of Dudley, a llama in the Rocky Mountains who constantly squabbles with his sibling. Pyjama-wearing llamas feature in L. Leslie Brooke's *Johnny Crow's New Garden* (1935), Mary Ann Hoberman's *The Llama Who Had No Pajama* (2006) and, perhaps most famously, Anna Dewdney's beautifully illustrated *Llama Llama Red Pyjama* (2005), which recounts the sorrowful tale of a young llama who misses his mama at bedtime. Another children's book, *Victor Vicuña's Volcano Vacation* (2012) by Barbara DeRubertis, narrates the adventures of a young

Even the Llamas
Put on Pyjamas.

Llamas sport pyjamas in L. Leslie Brooke's *Johnny Crow's New Garden* (1935).

vicuña, the eponymous Victor, who goes on an action-packed summer holiday with his raven friend, Nevva Moore.

Two of the most well-known poems about llamas play on the peculiar spelling of the animal's name and its phonetic similarity with that of the Dalai Lama. In his pithy *Ode to the Llama* (1940), the American poet Ogden Nash ponders the many meanings of the word 'llama', noting that a lama spelled with one 'l' is a 'priest', while llama spelled with two is a 'beast'. Taking the idea a step further, Nash wonders whether there is such a thing as a llama spelled with three 'ls', and concludes that there is not.[30] The joke for readers in the United States, however, is that the term 'three-alarmer' does exist: it is used to describe fires requiring the attendance of multiple crews.

Nash's nineteenth-century predecessor, Hilaire Belloc, expresses similar fascination with the llama's strange name in his illustrated poetry book *More Beasts (For Worse Children)* (1897). Like Nash, Belloc compares the camelid with his human counterpart, 'the Lord of Turkestan', giving the former the more favourable write-up. Belloc's poetry is inflected with the racial prejudices of his era:

The Llama is a woolly sort of fleecy hairy goat,
With an indolent expression and an undulating throat
Like an unsuccessful literary man.

And I know the place he lives in (or at least – I think I do)
It is Ecuador, Brazil or Chili – possibly Peru;
You must find it in the Atlas if you can.

The Llama of the Pampasses you never should confound
(In spite of a deceptive similarity of sound)
With a Lhama who is Lord of Turkestan.

For the former is a beautiful and valuable beast,
But the latter is not lovable nor useful in the least;
And the Ruminant is preferable surely to the Priest
Who battens on the woeful superstitions of the East,
The Mongol of the Monastery of Shan.[31]

More melancholic in tone is Gabriela Mistral's poem, 'The Alpaca' (1932), which describes a female alpaca serving as a beast of burden in the Andes. The poem presents the alpaca as a gentle, obedient but uncomprehending animal, who patiently awaits the return of her master and suffers in the heat under her unshorn fleece: 'Today, large scissors that will cut and cut represent mercy for the alpaca.' Mistral focuses on the animal's maternal qualities, describing her at one point as 'the mother alpaca' and emphasizing her place in childhood memories. She also returns repeatedly to the alpaca's beautiful but unreadable eyes, which appear 'full of strangeness', 'astonished' and 'without knowledge'. The final lines of the poem draw a parallel between the snowy-fleeced alpaca and the snow-capped Andean mountain, which is also 'casting off burdens' in the form of an avalanche. These allusions to 'the older alpaca' (the mountain) suggest that the alpaca is intimately connected to the Peruvian landscape, embodying the ancient spirit of the sierra.[32]

An earlier female writer, the French feminist and socialist Flora Tristan, offers a similarly sympathetic portrayal of llamas in her autobiography, *Peregrinations of a Pariah* (1838), which recounts her travels in newly independent Peru. In a rather poetic description, Tristan admires the animals' handsome physique, noting how their 'long majestic necks, shining silky coats and timid supple movements' give them 'an expression of nobility that commands respect'. She romanticizes the moral superiority of the llama, which 'will make itself useful only on condition that it is *asked*, and never *ordered*', and surmises from this noble behaviour that it is 'the only animal in the service of man which he does not strike'. In a passage full of pathos, Tristan alleges that a llama that is beaten will lie down and die on the spot, 'big tears fall[ing] from its beautiful eyes and sighs issu[ing] from its breast'. This propensity 'to accept life only on condition that it be sweet' is a quality it purportedly shares with the Peruvian Indian, who, according to Tristan, also possesses 'the moral strength to escape oppression through death'.[33]

In modern adult fiction, two of the most iconic camelid portrayals appear in the work of Peru's most famous novelist, Mario Vargas Llosa, and both concentrate on vicuñas. In Vargas Llosa's first novel, *La Ciudad y los perros* (1962, published in English as *The Time of the Hero*), a vicuña is an unexpected resident at a military college in Lima, where corruption, bullying and a rampant culture of masculinity lead to the murder of a young cadet. The vicuña's innocence and feminine features contrast with the aggressive masculinity of the cadets, while its displacement from the sierra to the coast symbolizes the isolation and alienation of some of the human characters. Like the boys, the vicuña is a solitary, melancholy figure, wrenched from its natural home and forced to adapt to a new and unnatural environment. Like them, it finds a way to survive, but never fully acclimatizes, going 'half mad' in the heat of the limeño summer. Appearing fleetingly throughout the novel, the vicuña reflects the different predicaments of the various characters and acts as a mirror for their private thoughts. One cadet, 'El Esclavo' ('The Slave'), himself an outcast, thinks the vicuña is 'a sad animal', friendless and alone in the world. Another, Cava, an Indian, observes how the vicuña endures the boys' taunts and stone-throwing impassively, without apparent fear or anger, a reaction he equates with the quiet stoicism of Peru's indigenous people.[34]

More harrowing is the scene in Vargas Llosa's later novel *Lituma en los Andes* (1993, published in English as *Death in the Andes*), where fighters in the Maoist guerrilla group Sendero Luminoso ('The Shining Path') brutally slaughter a flock of vicuñas in the Pampa Galeras reserve. Vargas Llosa narrates the massacre in lurid detail, describing how the timid, frightened animals fall before a hail of bullets, their bones shattered and 'their snouts, eyes and ears torn off by the projectiles'.[35] He accentuates the horror of the attack by presenting it through the eyes of the vicuñas' mute shepherd, Pedro Tinoco, who innocently leads the terrorists to the beasts' hideout and watches in traumatized silence as his flock is gunned down. The slaughter of the vicuñas foreshadows the subsequent murders of Indian villagers in the novel and underlines the callous cruelty of the guerrillas, who kill man and beast alike in cold blood. Though a work of fiction, the massacre is grounded in reality: Sendero Luminoso did assault vicuñas during their war against the Peruvian state, and *senderistas* murdered Barbara d'Achille, an Italianborn ecologist involved in vicuña conservation. It is thought that the vicuña population of Ayacucho halved from a total of 30,000 to 15,000 during the 1980s, the time when 'The Shining Path' was at its most active.[36]

As well as featuring in literature, llamas have had a presence on stage and screen since the early nineteenth century. In 1813 an alpaca starred in the popular pantomime *The Red Dwarf* in Covent Garden alongside the famous clown Grimaldi. In 1835 a llama from Liverpool Zoo performed in the pantomime *Bluebeard*, together with an elephant and a large dromedary (Arabian camel).[37] In both these cases, the relevance of llamas to the actual plot was tenuous, but their presence added a level of drama and interest to proceedings, giving circus visitors and theatregoers a taste of the exotic.

In the twentieth century, llamas have broken into film and television. The pushmi-pullyu in Hugh Lofting's *Dr Dolittle* (1920) is portrayed in the 1967 film adaptation as a two-headed llama (it was a gazelle–unicorn hybrid in the book), speaking with one head and eating with the other. More recently, an alpaca named Tina made a brief cameo in the quirky 2004 high school comedy *Napoleon Dynamite*, while another alpaca achieved notoriety in the modern-day Noah's Ark comedy *Evan Almighty* (2007) by spitting on a congressman (further evidence, by the way, that there *were* alpacas on the Ark). An expressive cartoon camelid appeared in Disney's Inca epic *The Emperor's New Groove* (2000), which sees the protagonist, Kuzco, turned into a llama by his evil advisor, Yzma. To animate the llama character correctly, the film's twelve animators studied llamas in zoos, went to visit a llama farm, watched nature documentaries and even had live llamas brought to the studio so they could examine their movements up close![38]

On television, llamas make an appearance in the BBC children's programme *Horrible Histories*, forming the subject of a song in an episode about the Incas. Two alpacas, Nuzzle and Scratch, appear in a drama of the same name on CBeebies (the BBC's channel for younger children), and three feisty llamas feature in Aardman Animation's Shaun the Sheep Christmas Special, *The Farmer's Llamas* (2015), wreaking havoc in the English countryside and exhibiting impressive football skills.

On the radio, two llamas, Constanza and Wolfgang (named in honour of Mozart and his wife), appeared in 2003 on the long-running BBC soap *The Archers*, which chronicles rural life in the fictional village of Ambridge. In 2007 Constanza gave birth to a *cria*, Salieri, and in 2013 Wolfgang died from bovine TB – a topical tragedy in light of contemporary debates about culling badgers to stop the spread of the disease.[39]

Llamas have also penetrated the world of advertising, often functioning as metaphors for Peru. A 1960s publicity campaign for Braniff International Airlines, publicizing flights to Peru,

An alpaca performs in 'the Popular Pantomime of the Red Dwarf' with the famous clown Grimaldi. R. Norman, 11 January 1813.

Alpaca chocolate, Arequipa, Peru.

features an indigenous man leading a grinning llama. A 1976 magazine advertisement for the spirit Pisco Llama is emblazoned with an image of a kind of llama-satyr, while a recruitment poster for the U.S. Navy depicts a beaming sailor feeding a banana to a llama. More recently, McVitie's have used alpacas to advertise a chocolate biscuit, in this case to embody the concept of 'sweetness'; Oxfam have run a campaign to buy alpacas for Peruvian farmers (the 'Alpaca Package'), with a catchy TV advert featuring toothy llamas; and the Australian power company Ergon have created a foreboding, black-caped character called the 'Grim Llama' to warn customers of the dangers of electricity. In Peru itself, several tour operators have adopted the name (and image) of the country's most iconic animals to attract foreign visitors on their holidays. Llamas and alpacas also appear on all manner of souvenirs, from fluffy toys to chocolate.

American sailors experience the 'inland sights' of Peru, including a llama, in this U.S. Navy recruitment poster from the First World War.

SOUTH AMERICA

COME ALONG
learn something, see something in the
U S NAVY
ample shore leave for inland sights

Two llamas advertise a remedy for altitude sickness, Pucará, Peru.

Llama souvenirs, Peru.

Finally, alpacas have recently hit the big time in the toy market, through the phenomenon of Alpacasso. Beginning in Japan around 2010, Alpacasso started as a series of fluffy toys, with curly fleeces and beguiling smiles. Made in a range of different colours and styles, the furry alpacas became a target for collectors, growing into something of a popular craze. From a stuffed toy, Alpacasso has evolved into a wider cultural phenomenon, spawning cartoons, animated songs and multiple online videos. An Australian TV company, Deerstalker Pictures, has even transformed Alpacasso into a TV chef, Señor Alpacasso, who teaches children how to make 'alpacaroons' (alpaca macaroons), crème brûlée and churros.

'Llama's Favourite Snack': Lloyd the llama consumes 'a hunk of cotton candy' at the Circus World Museum, Baraboo, U.S., 1965.

Since their domestication high in the Andes, llamas and alpacas have come a long way. They have been hunted, worshipped, farmed, smuggled and petted. They have functioned at different times as sacred beings, luxury commodities, literary muses and national symbols, and they have served by turns as sacrificial victims, pantomime performers, golf caddies, wedding guests and pasty fillings. From Peru to Australia, Bolivia to Japan, camelids have acquired a global presence and an international significance. With increased efforts to promote these wonderful animals both within and beyond South America, this reputation is only set to grow.

Timeline of the Llama

40–50 MYA	*c.* 3 MYA	4500 BC	*c.* 200 BC–AD 600
The first camelids appear in North America	Camelids migrate to South America	Earliest evidence for camelid domestication in South America	Llamas and alpacas appear on Nazca, Recuay and Moche ceramics

1770S	1808	1811	1827
The Spanish Crown passes further legislation to protect vicuñas	A troop of llamas and alpacas arrives in Cádiz, destined for the Empress Joséphine Bonaparte	First alpaca is exhibited in Britain	The Liberator Simón Bolívar issues a decree banning the killing of vicuñas

1858	1907		1967
Charles Ledger imports 256 alpacas into Australia	A. W. Wingfield rides llamas at his menagerie in Bedfordshire		First reserve for vicuñas established at Pampa Galeras, Peru

1400–1532	1557	1558	c. 1750

Llamas and alpacas play a central role in Inca culture

The Spanish Crown imposes a five-year moratorium on vicuña hunting

First llama exhibited in Europe

Vicuña wool becomes popular in Europe as a luxury fibre

1830s	1840s	1845	1846

Titus Salt begins manufacturing alpaca wool in Bradford

Britain imports alpacas

Peru prohibits the export of alpacas

Peruvian priest Juan Pablo Cabrera breeds paco-vicuñas at Macusani

1984	1993	2012	2014

International Alpaca Association founded in Arequipa

Peru permits the export of llamas and alpacas

Peru holds the first National Alpaca Day on 1 August

Bolivia petitions the UN to name 2016 'Year of the Camelid'

References

INTRODUCTION

1 Edward Topsell, *The historie of foure-footed beastes . . . collected out of all the volumes of Conradus Gesner, and all other writers to this present day* (London, 1607), p. 102.

1 ALPACAS UNPACKED

1 Robert Irwin, *Camel* (London, 2010), pp. 36–45; Jane Wheeler, 'Evolution and Present Situation of the South American Camelidae', *Biological Journal of the Linnaean Society*, LIV (1995), pp. 271–95.
2 Nick Saunders, 'The Civilising Influence of Agriculture', *New Scientist* (13 June 1985), pp. 16–18; Guillermo Luis Mengoni Goñalons, 'Camelids in Ancient Andean Societies: A Review of the Zooarcheological Evidence', *Quaternary International*, CLXXXV (2008), pp. 59–68.
3 Juan de Velasco, *Historia del reino de Quito en la América meridional* (Quito, 1841), vol. I, pt I, p. 82.
4 Zoological Society of London, *The Gardens and Menagerie of the Zoological Society Delineated*, vol. I, 'Quadrupeds' (Chiswick, 1830), p. 279.
5 Miranda Kadwell, Jane Wheeler et al., 'Genetic Analysis Reveals the Wild Ancestors of the Llama and the Alpaca', *Proceedings of the Royal Society, London*, 268 (2001), pp. 2575–85.

6 Kent Flannery, Joyce Marcus and Robert Reynolds, *The Flocks of the Wamani: A Study of Llama Herders on the Punas of Ayacucho, Peru* (San Diego, CA, 1980), pp. 94–5.

7 'Alpaca Information', www.sunsetalpacas.co.nz, accessed 7 December 2015.

8 A micron is 1/1,000 mm.

9 Kim MacQuarrie, *Gold of the Andes: The Llamas, Alpacas, Vicuñas and Guanacos of South America* (Barcelona, 1995), pp. 120–21.

10 Marcelo Cassini, Mariela Borgina, Yanina Arzamendia, Verónica Benítez and Bibianna Vilá, 'Sociality, Foraging and Habitat Use by Vicuña', in *The Vicuña: The Theory and Practice of Community-based Wildlife Management*, ed. Iain Gordon (New York, 2009), p. 41.

11 William Walton, *A Memoir Addressed to Proprietors of Mountain and other Waste Lands and Agriculturalists of the United Kingdom, on the Naturalisation of the Alpaca* (London, 1841), p. 21.

12 Alex Chepstow-Lusty, 'Agro-pastoralism and Social Change in the Cuzco Heartland of Peru: A Brief History using Environmental Proxies', *Antiquity*, LXXXV (2011), p. 579.

13 Charles Ledger, 'The Alpaca', in George Bennett, MD, FLS, *The Third Annual Report of the Acclimatisation Society of New South Wales* (Sydney, 1864), pp. 92–3.

14 *Adelaide Observer* (25 September 1858).

15 Amédée Frézier, *Voyage de la mer du sud au côtes du Chili et du Pérou*, ed. Gaston Arduz Eguía et Hubert Michéa (Thizy, 1995), p. 165.

16 Ledger, 'The Alpaca', p. 92.

17 Bruce W. Brown, 'A Review of Reproduction in South American Camelids', *Animal Reproduction Science*, LVIII (2000), pp. 169–95.

18 'Meet Rama the Cama . . .', www.bbc.co.uk, 21 January 1998.

2 SUSTENANCE AND SACRIFICE

1 José M. Capriles and Nicolás Tripcerich, *The Archaeology of Andean Pastoralism* (Albuquerque, NM, 2016).

2 Charles Ledger, 'The Alpaca', in George Bennett, MD, FLS,
   *The Third Annual Report of the Acclimatisation Society of New South
   Wales* (Sydney, 1864), pp. 92–3.

3 Bernabé Cobo, *Historia del nuevo mundo* (Seville, 1895), vol. IV,
   p. 156.

4 Cristóbal de Molina, *Account of the Fables and Rites of the Incas*
   (Austin, TX, 2011), p. 21.

5 Garcilaso de la Vega, *Primera parte de los comentarios reales*
   (Madrid, 1829), p. 355.

6 Karen Spalding, *Huarochirí: An Andean Society under Inca and
   Spanish Rule* (Stanford, CA, 1984), p. 16.

7 Cobo, *Historia*, vol. IV, p. 203.

8 José de Acosta, *Natural and Moral History of the Indies*, ed. Jane
   Mangan, trans. Frances López-Morillas (Durham, NC, 2002),
   p. 244.

9 Martín de Murúa, *Historia general del Perú* (Madrid, 2001), p. 457.

10 Alcide d'Orbigny and Paul Gervais, *Voyage dans l'Amérique
   Méridionale, executé pendant les années 1826, 1827, 1828, 1829,
   1830, 1831, 1832 et 1833*, vol. I: *'L'Homme Américain* (Paris, 1838–9),
   pp. 99–100.

11 Cobo, *Historia*, vol. IV, p. 205.

12 Ibid., p. 173.

13 Terence N. D'Altroy, *The Incas* (London, 2003), p. 409.

14 Cobo, *Historia*, vol. IV, pp. 117–18.

15 Clements R. Markham, ed. and trans., *The Travels of Pedro Cieza
   de León, AD 1532–50, Contained in the First Part of his Chronicle of
   Peru* (London, 1864), vol. I, p. 395n.

16 Cobo, *Historia*, vol. IV, pp. 229, 159.

17 Andrés Chirinos and Martha Zegarra, eds, *El Orden del Inca, por
   el licenciado Polo Ondegardo* (Lima, 2013), p. 115.

18 Cobo, *Historia*, vol. II, pp. 321–3.

19 D'Altroy, *The Incas*, p. 342.

20 Chirinos and Zegarra, *El Orden del Inca*, p. 115.

21 D'Altroy, *The Incas*, p. 408.

22 Chirinos and Zegarra, *El Orden del Inca*, p. 113.

23 Markham, *The Travels of Pedro Cieza de León*, vol. I, p. 395n.

24 Ibid.

25 Chirinos and Zegarra, *El Orden del Inca*, pp. 117, 119.

26 Markham, *The Travels of Pedro Cieza de León*, vol. II, pp. 45–6.

27 De la Vega, *Comentarios reales*, pp. 447–9.

28 William Walton, *The Alpaca: Its Naturalisation in the British Isles Considered as a National Benefit, and as an Object of Immediate Utility to the Farmer and Manufacturer* (New York, 1845), p. 6.

29 Mariano Rivero, *Antiguedades Peruanas* (Vienna, 1851), p. 195.

30 Cobo, *Historia*, vol. IV, pp. 96, 104, 108.

31 Ledger, 'The Alpaca', p. 94.

32 Cobo, *Historia*, vol. IV, pp. 96–7.

33 Molina, *Fables and Rites*, p. 56.

34 Claudia Brosseder, *The Power of the Huacas: Change and Resistance in the Andean World of Colonial Peru* (Austin, TX, 2014), pp. 170–71.

35 Cobo, *Historia*, vol. IV, pp. 108, 118–19.

36 'Drawing 99. The tenth month, October; *Uma Raymi Killa*, month of the principal feast', from Felipe Guamán Poma, *El Nuevo corónica y buen Gobierno* (1615), 'The Guaman Poma Website', www.kb.dk, accessed 7 December 2015.

37 Cobo, *Historia*, vol. IV, p. 117.

38 De la Vega, *Comentarios reales*, pp. 496–7. In another similar ritual the Incas sacrificed a black male llama in preparation for a military campaign, having kept the animal 'in prison without eating' for several days prior to the sacrifice. If 'a certain piece of flesh behind the [llama's] heart' was found not to have been consumed by the fasting process, this was taken as a bad omen, and some black dogs were sacrificed and eaten to pacify the gods. Murúa, *Historia general del Perú*, p. 409.

39 Kenneth Mills, *Idolatry and its Enemies: Colonial Andean Religion and Extirpation, 1640–1750* (Princeton, NJ, 1997), p. 78.

40 Rivero, *Antiguedades Peruanas*, p. 170.

41 Mills, *Idolatry and its Enemies*, p. 78.

42 Pablo José de Arriaga, *Extirpación de la idolatria del Perú* (Lima, 1621), p. 129.

43 Frank Salomon and George L. Urioste, eds and trans, *The Huarochirí Manuscript: A Testament of Ancient and Colonial Andean Religion* (Austin, TX, 1991), pp. 51–2.

44 Ibid., pp. 132–3.

45 De la Vega, *Comentarios reales*, p. 161. On the role of animals in Inca astrology, see Gary Urton, 'Animals and Astronomy in the Quechua Universe', *Proceedings of the American Philosophical Society*, CXXV/2 (1981), pp. 110–27.

3 PERUVIAN SHEEP

1 Antonio Pigafetta, *Primer viaje en torno del globo* [1536] (Madrid, 2004), p. 80.

2 José de Acosta, *Natural and Moral History of the Indies*, ed. Jane Mangan, trans. Frances López-Morillas (Durham, NC, 2002), pp. 244 and 242; Clements R. Markham, ed. and trans., *The Travels of Pedro Cieza de León, AD 1532–50, Contained in the First Part of his Chronicle of Peru* (London, 1864), vol. I, p. 393.

3 *Relaciones geográficas de Indias*, vol. II, Peru (Madrid, 1885), p. 76. The *Relaciones geográficas* were responses to a set of questions sent out by Philip II in the mid-sixteenth century requesting information about the flora, fauna and topography of the new Spanish colonies and the customs and beliefs of their inhabitants. For further discussion of llamas in the *Relaciones geográficas*, see Abel Alves, *The Animals of Spain: An Introduction to Imperial Perceptions and Human Interaction with Other Animals, 1492–1826* (Leiden, 2011), pp. 105 and 204.

4 See Miguel Asúa and Roger French, *A New World of Animals: Early Modern Europeans on the Creatures of Iberoamerica* (Aldershot, 2005), p. 14. Interestingly, the Incas initially called Spanish horses 'llamas, which is how we call our livestock . . . since we had never seen any before', so the process worked both ways. See Diego de Castro Yupangui, Titu Cussi, *An Inca Account of the Conquest of Peru*, trans. Ralph Bauer (Boulder, CO, 2005), p. 61.

5 George Marcgrave and Willem Piso, *Historia naturalis Brasiliae* (Amsterdam, 1648), p. 244.

6 Edward Topsell, *The historie of foure-footed beastes . . . collected out of all the volumes of Conradus Gesner, and all other writers to this present day* (London, 1607), p. 102.

7 William Prescott, *History of the Conquest of Peru* (London, 1890), p. 144.

8 Zoological Society of London, *The Gardens and Menagerie of the Zoological Society Delineated*, vol. I, 'Quadrupeds' (Chiswick, 1830), p. 280.

9 Acosta, *Natural and Moral History of the Indies*, p. 245.

10 Antonio de Léon Pinelo, *El Paraíso en el nuevo mundo* (Lima, 1943), vol. II, p. 53.

11 Acosta, *Natural and Moral History of the Indies*, p. 246.

12 Bernabé Cobo, *Historia del nuevo mundo* (Seville, 1895), vol. II, p. 321.

13 Markham, *The Travels of Pedro Cieza de León*, vol. I, p. 394.

14 Acosta, *Natural and Moral History of the Indies*, p. 243.

15 Garcilaso de la Vega, *Primera Parte de los Comentarios Reales* (Madrid, 1829), p. 430.

16 Gaspar de Escalona Agüero, *Gazofilacio Real del Peru* (La Paz, 1941), p. 264.

17 Acosta, *Natural and Moral History of the Indies*, p. 243.

18 Markham, *The Travels of Pedro Cieza de León*, p. 393; Léon Pinelo, *El Paraíso en el Nuevo Mundo*, vol. II, p. 53.

19 On the arrival of Old World animals in the Americas, see Alfred Crosby, *The Columbian Exchange: Biological and Cultural Consequences of 1492* (Westport, CT, 1972); and Elinor Melville, *A Plague of Sheep: Environmental Consequences of the Conquest of Mexico* (Cambridge, 1994). On the relationship between diet and ethnic identity in colonial Spanish America, see Rebecca Earle, *The Body of the Conquistador: Food, Race and the Colonial Experience in Spanish America, 1492–1700* (Cambridge, 2012).

20 Prescott, *History of the Conquest of Peru*, p. 365.

21 Acosta, *Natural and Moral History of the Indies*, p. 243.

22 Cobo, *Historia*, vol. II, p. 323; Adam Warren, 'From Natural History to Popular Remedy: Animals and their Medicinal Applications

among the Kallawaya in Colonial Peru', in Martha Few and Zeb
Tortorici, eds, *Centering Animals in Latin American History*
(Chapel Hill, NC, 2014), p. 141.

23 Nicolás Monardes, *Primera, segunda y tercera parte de la historia
medicina* (Seville, 1574), pp. 74–7.

24 Acosta, *Natural and Moral History of the Indies*, p. 248; Léon Pinelo,
El Paraíso en el nuevo mundo, vol. II, p. 271.

25 Asúa and French, *A New World of Animals*, p. 92.

26 Monardes, *Primera, segunda y tercera parte de la historia medicina*,
pp. 74–7.

27 Ibid., p. 112.

28 On the importance of experience in understanding New World
fauna and flora, and the resulting epistemological shifts, see
Antonio Barrera-Osorio, *Experiencing Nature: The Spanish American
Empire and the Early Scientific Revolution* (Austin, TX, 2006).

29 Acosta, *Natural and Moral History of the Indies*, pp. 235–6.

30 Athanasius Kircher, *Arca Noë in tres libros digesta* (Amsterdam,
1675), pp. 67–73.

31 Pablo José de Arriaga, *Extirpación de la idolatria del Perú*
(Lima, 1621), p. 45.

32 Kenneth Mills, *Idolatry and its Enemies: Colonial Andean Religion
and Extirpation, 1640–1750* (Princeton, NJ, 1997), pp. 63, 66, 263.

33 Martín de Murúa, *Historia general del Perú* (Madrid, 2001), p. 443.

34 Lorenz Fries, *Uselegung der Mercarthen oder Carta Marina*
(Strasbourg, 1525), leaf XVI, Archive of Early American Images,
The John Carter Brown Library.

35 Prescott, *History of the Conquest of Peru*, p. 203.

36 Murúa, *Historia general del Perú*, p. 558.

37 De la Vega, *Comentarios reales*, p. 352.

38 Acosta, *Natural and Moral History of the Indies*, p. 242.

39 Hugo Yacobaccio, 'The Historical Relationship between People
and the Vicuña', in Iain Gordon, ed., *The Vicuña: The Theory and*

Practice of Community-based Wildlife Management (New York, 2009), p. 14.

40 Hipólito Ruiz, *The Journals of Hipólito Ruíz, Spanish Botanist in Peru and Chile, 1777–1788*, trans. Richard Evans Schultes and María José Nemry von Thenen de Jaramillo-Arango (Portland, OR, 1998), p. 104.

41 Markham, *The Travels of Pedro Cieza de León*, vol. I, p. 393; Girolamo Benzoni, *History of the New World* (London, 1857), p. 249.

42 Andrés Chirinos and Martha Zegarra, eds, *El Orden del Inca, por el licenciado Polo Ondegardo* (Lima, 2013), p. 117.

43 De la Vega, *Comentarios reales*, p. 352.

44 Jane Wheeler, 'Evolution and Present Situation of the South American Camelidae', *Biological Journal of the Linnaean Society*, LIV (1995), pp. 271–95.

4 ENLIGHTENED LLAMAS

1 Pedro Franco Dávila, *Instrucción hecha de orden del Rey N. S. para que los virreyes, gobernadores, corregidores, alcaldes mayores e intendentes de provincias en todos los dominios de S. M. puedan hacer escoger, preparar y enviar a Madrid todas las producciones curiosas de naturaleza que se encontraren en las tierras y pueblos de sus distritos, a fin de que se coloquen en el Real Gabinete de Historia Natural que S. M. ha establecido en esta Corte para beneficio e instrucción pública* (Madrid, 1776), p. 4. On the Bourbon Reforms and their impact on the natural sciences, see Helen Cowie, *Conquering Nature in Spain and its Empire* (Manchester, 2011).

2 Archivo General de Indias (AGI), Indiferente 1549.

3 'Lama', in Etienne Geoffroy de Saint-Hilaire and Frédéric Cuvier, *Histoire naturelle des mammifères* (Paris, 1824), vol. II, p. 2.

4 'Chameau' in Jean-Victor Audouin and Isidore Bourdon, *Dictionnaire classique d'histoire naturelle* (Paris, 1822–31), vol. III, p. 447.

5 Hipólito Ruíz, *The Journals of Hipólito Ruíz, Spanish Botanist in Peru and Chile, 1777–1788*, trans. Richard Evans Schultes and María José Nemry von Thenen de Jaramillo-Arango (Portland, OR, 1998), p. 105.

6 Georges-Louis Leclerc, Comte de Buffon, *Histoire naturelle générale et particulière* (Paris, 1765), vol. XIII, pp. 16–33.

7 Juan Ignacio Molina, *Compendio de la historia geográfica, natural y civíl del reyno de Chile* (Madrid, 1788), pp. 350–64.

8 'De las Vicuñas', *Semanario de agricultura y artes dirigido a los Parrócos* (1801), vol. X, p. 263.

9 *Semanario de agricultura, industria y comercio*, vol. II/72 (February 1804), p. 176, and vol. III/103 (September 1804), p. 7.

10 Hugo Yacobaccio, 'The Historical Relationship between People and the Vicuña', in Iain Gordon, ed., *The Vicuña: The Theory and Practice of Community-based Wildlife Management* (New York, 2009), p. 12.

11 'Real Cédula a la Audiencia de Charcas, para que cuide de que no se hagan cazerías en que se maten las vicuñas' (30 August 1777), *Documentos para la historia del Río de la plata* (Buenos Aires, 1913), vol. III, pp. 40–41.

12 AGI Lima 652.24; AGI Lima 651.59; AGI Lima 652.24; AGI Lima 652.182; AGI Indiferente 1549, 'Vicuñas', A Parrot joined the camelids on their journey'.

13 'Chameau', in Audouin and Bourdon, *Dictionnaire classique d'histoire naturelle*, vol. III, pp. 454–5; Museo Nacional de Ciencias Naturales, Fondo Zoológico, Sección Sociedad de Aclimatación, legajo 329/003.

14 Molina, *Compendio*, pp. 350–64. Jesuit natural histories shifted from universal natural histories in the sixteenth and seventeenth centuries to more localized natural histories in the eighteenth century, reflecting the growth of regional identities. See Silvia Navia Méndez-Bonito, 'Las historias naturales de Francisco Javier Clavijero, Juan Ignacio Molina y Juan de Velasco', in Luís Millones

Figueroa and Domingo Ledezma, eds, *El Saber de los Jesuitas: historias naturales y el nuevo mundo* (Frankfurt, 2005), p. 228.

15 'Sobre la posibilidad de domesticar a la Vicuña, cruzar su casta con las de la Llama, la Oveja y el Guanaco, y medios que debían tentarse para conseguirlo', *Semanario de agricultura, industria y comercio*, III/138 (May 1805), pp. 283–7.

16 Francisco José de Caldas, 'Memoria sobre la importancia de connaturalizar en el reino la vicuña del Perú y Chile', in *Obras completas de Francisco José de Caldas* (Bogotá, 1966), pp. 323–33.

17 Peter Flindell-Klarén, *Peru: Society and Nationhood in the Andes* (New York, 2000), p. 166.

18 *Sydney Morning Herald* (21 August 1860).

19 'Paper read by Charles Ledger at the Acclimatisation Society of New South Wales on 26 January 1864', in George Bennett, *The Third Annual Report of the Acclimatisation Society of New South Wales* (Sydney, 1864), p. 93.

20 Pierre-Amédée Pichot, *Le Jardin d'acclimatation illustré: animaux et plantes* (Paris, 1873), p. 79.

21 *El Comercio* (13 August 1845); *The Era* (25 September 1859).

22 *El Comercio* (8 April 1851); *Decreto Estableciendo la prohibición de extraer del territorio peruano las alpacas, vicuñas y animales que proceden del cruzamiento de ambas razas*, 8 October 1868, Archivo Digital de la Legislación del Perú.

23 *El Peruano* (9 September 1846). Similar rewards were offered to individuals who introduced alpacas to areas of the country where they had not previously been farmed. In 1845, for instance, a reward of 250 pesos was offered to anyone who introduced alpacas to the department of Junín, with a further 25 pesos for every 50 *crias* bred in the region. *Suplemento al Peruano*, 7 October 1845.

24 MNCN, Fondo Zoológico, Sección Sociedad de Aclimatación, legajo 328/019.

25 Augusto Fauvety, *Primera introducción de alpacas y llamas en la república oriental del Uruguay* (Montevideo, 1867), pp. 10–13.

26 Georges-Louis Leclerc, Comte de Buffon, *Buffon's Natural History* (London, 1797), p. 27.

27 Cornelius de Pauw, *Récherches philosophiques sur les Américains* (London, 1770), vol. I, pp. 7–13.

28 Molina, *Compendio*, p. 353.

29 'Memoria sobre la importancia de connaturalizar en el reino la vicuña del Perú y Chile', in Caldas, *Obras completas*, p. 324; Hipólito Unánue, *Observaciones sobre el clima de Lima* (Lima, 1806), p. 94.

30 Mark Thurner, 'Peruvian Genealogies of History and Nation', in Mark Thurner and Andrés Guerrero, eds, *After Spanish Rule: Postcolonial Predicaments of the Americas* (Durham, NC, 2003), pp. 141–76; Rebecca Earle, *The Return of the Native: Indians and Myth-making in Spanish America, 1810–1930* (Durham, NC, 2007).

31 *Caledonian Mercury* (26 January 1826).

5 FROM THE ANDES TO THE OUTBACK

1 William Walton, *The Alpaca: Its Naturalisation in the British Isles Considered as a National Benefit, and as an Object of Immediate Utility to the Farmer and Manufacturer* (New York, 1845), p. 15; *Extraordinary Living Rarities, Exhibiting for a Few Days Longer at 236, Piccadilly*, John Johnson Collection of Printed Ephemera (Animals on Show), 2 (52).

2 Important studies of this phenomenon include Lucille Brockway, *Science and Colonial Expansion: The Role of the British Royal Botanic Gardens* (New Haven, CT, 2002); Richard Drayton, *Nature's Government: Science, Imperial Britain and the 'Improvement' of the World* (New Haven, CT, 2000); and Londa Schiebinger, *Plants and Empire: Colonial Bio-prospecting in the Atlantic World* (Cambridge, MA, 2004).

3 *Morning Chronicle* (21 March 1805).
4 William Walton, *A Memoir Addressed to Proprietors of Mountain and other Waste Lands and Agriculturalists of the United Kingdom, on the Naturalisation of the Alpaca* (London, 1841), p. 22.
5 London zoo possessed a white and a brown llama in 1829. The former was described as 'gentle, mild and familiar' and the latter as 'morose'. *Guide to the Gardens of the Zoological Society* (London, 1829), pp. 8–9.
6 *Ipswich Journal* (30 April 1814).
7 William Danson, *Alpaca, The Original Peruvian Sheep, Before the Spaniards Invaded South America, for Naturalisation in other Countries. Recommended through the Natural History Society of Liverpool in 1839* (Liverpool, 1852), p. 7.
8 George Ledger, *The Alpaca: Its Introduction into Australia and the Probabilities of its Acclimatisation There. A Paper read before the Society of Arts, London*. Republished by the Acclimatisation Society of Victoria (Melbourne, 1861), p. 5.
9 Walton, *The Alpaca*, p. 12; Walton, *Memoir*, p. 19; Walton, *The Alpaca*, p. 11 and pp. 7–8 and 13; Danson, *Alpaca*, p. 19.
10 *Morning Chronicle* (30 September 1840); *Caledonian Mercury* (12 August 1844); Walton, *The Alpaca*, pp. 14–19.
11 Walton, *Memoir*, p. 23.
12 Walton, *The Alpaca*, p. 19.
13 Walton, *Memoir*, p. 23.
14 On the tradition of animal husbandry and the fashion for fat cattle in nineteenth-century Britain, see 'Barons of Beef' in Harriet Ritvo, *The Animal Estate: The English and Other Creatures in the Victorian Age* (Cambridge, MA, 1987), pp. 45–81.
15 Walton, *The Alpaca*, pp. 16, 17, 21 and 15.
16 *Freeman's Journal* (13 August 1858); Linden Gillbank, 'A Paradox of Purposes: Acclimatization Origins of the Melbourne Zoo', in R. J. Hoage and William A. Deiss, *New Worlds, New Animals: From Menagerie to Zoological Park in the Nineteenth Century* (Baltimore, MD, 1996), pp. 76–9.
17 *Bradford Observer* (28 July 1864).

18 Paper read by Charles Ledger to the Australian Agricultural Society, reprinted in *Bradford Observer* (29 September 1859).

19 Ledger, *The Alpaca*, pp. 11–13.

20 *The Era* (20 February 1859).

21 Ibid. (25 September 1859).

22 *Bradford Observer* (29 September 1859).

23 *The Era* (12 February 1860).

24 *Sydney Morning Herald* (28 June 1865).

25 Ibid. (29 February 1864).

26 *The Era* (12 February 1860); *Bradford Observer* (28 July 1864).

27 Henry Southern, HM Minister at Rio, presented the Zoological Society of London with a tapir in 1853. W. D. Christie, HM Minister to the Argentine Confederation, presented 'a pair of pumas' in 1857. See *Report of the Council and Auditors of the Zoological Gardens of London* (London, 1853), p. 18; ibid. (London, 1857), p. 19.

28 For a detailed study of British and Irish ex-soldiers in Colombia, Venezuela and Ecuador, see Matthew Brown, *Adventuring through Spanish Colonies: Simón Bolívar, Foreign Mercenaries and the Birth of New Nations* (Liverpool, 2006).

29 Walton, *The Alpaca*, p. 28.

30 *Sydney Morning Herald* (7 November 1859).

31 Ibid. (21 August 1860).

32 Walton, *The Alpaca*, p. 6.

33 *Maitland Mercury* (20 March 1850)

34 *Liverpool Mercury* (1 October 1841).

35 *Bradford Observer* (29 September 1859).

36 Danson, *Alpaca*, pp. 12–14.

37 Ibid., p. 20.

38 Walton, *Memoir*, p. 20.

39 Walton, *The Alpaca*, p. 11.

40 Danson, *Alpaca*, p. 19.

41 *Daily News* (8 November 1858); Walton, *The Alpaca*, p. 15; Walton, *Memoir*, pp. 21–3.

42 Walton, *Memoir*, p. 23.

43 *Liverpool Mercury* (2 and 11 February and 22 March 1853). On travelling menageries in the Victorian era, see Helen Cowie, *Exhibiting Animals in Nineteenth-century Britain: Empathy, Education, Entertainment* (Basingstoke, 2014).

44 William Haines, chairing the meeting at which George Ledger advocated alpaca introduction into Australia, emphasized 'the importance of promoting increased production of wool when our supply of cotton might be in danger'. See Ledger, *The Alpaca*, p. 24.

45 Danson, *Alpaca*, pp. 12–14.

46 *Morning Chronicle* (14 December 1844); *Leeds Mercury* (12 April 1845); *Leeds Mercury* (21 May 1859).

47 *The Times* (17 July 1858).

48 *The Era* (25 September 1859).

49 Ibid. (23 November 1862).

50 Walton, *The Alpaca*, p. 15; Augusto Fauvety, *Primera introducción de alpacas y llamas en la república oriental del Uruguay* (Montevideo, 1867), p. 9.

51 Museo Nacional de Ciencias Naturales (MNCN), Fondo Zoológico, Sección Sociedad de Aclimatación, legajo 328/019.

52 Pierre-Amédée Pichot, *Le Jardin d'acclimatation illustré: animaux et plantes* (Paris, 1873), pp. 5–8 and 79.

53 M. E. Deville, *Considérations sur les avantages de la naturalisation en france de l'alpaca* (Paris, 1851), p. 15; Société Impériale Zoologique D'Acclimatation, Fondée à Paris, le 14 Février 1854 (Paris, no date), p. 7.

54 Michael Osborne, *Nature, the Exotic and the Science of French Colonialism* (Bloomington, IN, 1994), pp. 134–6.

55 Ledger, *The Alpaca*, p. ii.

56 In 1882, for instance, Cross advertised '1 pair adult llamas' and '1 pure white alpaca'. *The Era* (22 December 1882).

57 *The Telegraph* (Brisbane) (5 June 1909). The surviving alpacas in Australia experienced a similar descent from promising export to exotic curiosity. In 1869, for instance, Thomas Lee exhibited 'a flock of twenty alpacas' at the Bathurst Agricultural Show, where the

'rare and beautiful animals' attracted 'a great deal of attention' but were not eligible for a prize. *Sydney Morning Herald* (30 April 1869).

58 *Singleton Argus* (17 April 1875).

6 A VERY MODERN LLAMA

1 Mariana Vega, TED *Case Studies*, number 667 (2002), www1.american.edu/ted/alpaca.htm, accessed 7 December 2015.

2 'Camelid Clips', International Alpaca Association, *Alpaca Monthly News* (September 2013), p. 2.

3 Pedro Moreno Vasquez, '26 Crazy Facts a Peruvian Wants you to Know about Llamas', www.xpatnation.com, 8 April 2016.

4 Jorge Flores-Ochoa, *Pastoralists of the Andes: The Alpaca Herders of Paratía* (Philadelphia, PA, 1979), pp. 71–85.

5 International Alpaca Association, 'About Us', http://aia.org.pe/en, accessed 30 November 2016.

6 Information available at http://docs.peru.justia.com/federales/leyes/28041-jul-23-2003.pdf, accessed 11 December 2016.

7 International Alpaca Association, *Alpaca Monthly News* (January 2013), p. 1.

8 Ibid., p. 3.

9 Dan Collyns, 'Alpacas get a Genetic Helping Hand', www.bbc.co.uk, 23 October 2006.

10 'Bolivia: The Alpaca Connection', http://webtv.un.org, 23 May 2013.

11 Bolivia, *International Year of the Camelids 2016*, U.N. General Assembly, Draft Resolution A/C.2/69/L.41 (7 November 2014).

12 Hernán Torres, ed., *South American Camelids: An Action Plan for their Conservation* (Gland, IUCN Species Survival Commission, 1992), p. 3.

13 Katarzyna Nowak, 'Legalizing Rhino Horn Trade Won't Save Species, Ecologist Argues. What can South Africa's Rhino Horn Trade Proponents Learn from Experiences with the South American Vicuña?', *National Geographic* (8 January 2015).

14 Cristian Bonacic, Jessica Gimpel and Pete Goddard, 'Animal
    Welfare and Sustainable Use of the Vicuña', in *The Vicuña:
    The Theory and Practice of Community-based Wildlife Management*,
    ed. Iain Gordon (New York, 2009), p. vii; International Alpaca
    Association, *Alpaca Monthly News* (September 2013), pp. 49–62.
15 Nowak, 'Legalizing Rhino Horn Trade'.
16 International Alpaca Association, *Alpaca Monthly News*
    (February 2014), p. 4.
17 Inca Alpaca, 'FAQ', www.incaalpaca.co.uk, accessed 7 December
    2015; Prue Adams, 'Meat the Alpacas: Fluffy, Cute, but Tasty',
    www.abc.net.au, 28 July 2013; 'How Many Alpaca are there in NZ?,
    New Zealand Alpaca (August 2012), pp. 26–7.
18 'Some Quaint Mounts', *The Bystander* (7 August 1907); *Punch*
    (7 April 1909).
19 Adams, 'Meat the Alpacas'.
20 Australian Alpaca Association, *La Viandé Australian Alpaca: Carcase
    and Cut Specifications* (Rural Industry Research and Development
    Corporation, 2007).
21 'Alpacas as Guardians', *International Camelid Quarterly*
    (September 2008).
22 Australian Alpaca Association, *Alpaca Fact Sheet #6* (2008).
23 Margo DeMello, *Animals and Society: An Introduction to
    Human-animal Studies* (New York, 2012), pp. 204–7.
24 Jennifer Kingson, 'The Llama Is In', *New York Times* (3 July 2013).
25 Letter from Thomas Holt to Sir Henry Parkes, 23 May 1873, State
    Library of New South Wales. *Sir Henry Parkes Papers, 1833–1896*,
    p. 366.
26 'Alpaca Shows and Events', www.bas-uk.com, accessed
    7 December 2015.
27 *Daily Mail* (16 July 2015). The first alpacas were imported into
    Japan in 1999. Tochigi has the country's largest alpaca farm,
    with over 400 animals. The public can visit and feed the alpacas,
    some of which have patterns shorn into their fur. A white female
    alpaca called Hanako 'wears a cute hat and has a basket hanging
    from her neck and poses for photos with visitors'. Reiko Senna,

'The Largest Alpaca Farm in Japan', http://en.japantravel.com, 21 April 2014.

28 Kim Willsher, 'Serge the Llama Rides Tram after being Abducted by Revellers in Bordeaux', *The Guardian* (4 November 2013); and 'Serge le lama assistera au match Bordeaux–Nantes', *Le Matin* (8 November 2013).

29 BBC Trending, 'Twitter Captivated by Arizona Llama Drama', www.bbc.co.uk, 26 February 2015.

30 Ogden Nash, 'Ode to the Llama', *The Face is Familiar* (London, 1942), p. 228.

31 Hilaire Belloc, *More Beasts (for Worse Children)* (London, 1897), pp. 239–42.

32 Gabriela Mistral, 'The Alpaca', in *Gabriela Mistral: Selected Prose and Prose-poems*, ed. Stephen Tapscott (Austin, TX, 2002), p. 21.

33 Flora Tristán, *Peregrinations of a Pariah*, ed. and trans. Jean Hawkes (London, 1986), pp. 131–2.

34 Mario Vargas Llosa, *La Ciudad y los Perros* (Madrid, 2006), pp. 418, 157, 18.

35 Mario Vargas Llosa, *Lituma en los Andes* (Barcelona, 2010), p. 51.

36 Matt Moffett, 'Después de Sendero . . . A Proteger Vicuñas', www.eltiempo.com, 13 June 1997.

37 *Grimaldi and the Alpaca, in the Popular Pantomime of the Red Dwarf, now performing with unbounded applause at the Theatre Royal, Covent Garden* (London, 1813); *Liverpool Mercury* (27 November 1835).

38 'The Emperor's New Groove', www.cinemareview.com, accessed 7 December 2015.

39 In 2014 researchers developed a blood test for TB in alpacas which can prove with 97 per cent accuracy whether or not an animal carries the disease. The £100,000 research project was financed entirely by UK alpaca owners, and may also prove suitable for testing cattle and badgers. See Philip Bowern, 'New Test for Alpacas Hailed a Breakthrough in Bovine TB Battle', *Western Morning News* (18 July 2014).

Bibliography

Acosta, José de, *Natural and Moral History of the Indies*, ed. Jane
    Mangan, trans. Frances López-Morillas (Durham, NC, 2002)
D'Altroy, Terence N., *The Incas* (London, 2003)
Alves, Abel, *The Animals of Spain: An Introduction to Imperial Perceptions
    and Human Interaction with Other Animals, 1492–1826* (Leiden, 2011)
Asúa, Miguel, and Roger French, *A New World of Animals: Early
    Modern Europeans on the Creatures of Iberoamerica* (Aldershot,
    2005)
Brown, Bruce W., 'A Review of Reproduction in South American
    Camelids', *Animal Reproduction Science*, LVIII (2000), pp. 169–95
Caldas, Francisco José de, 'Memoria sobre la importancia de
    connaturalizar en el reino la vicuña del Perú y Chile', in *Obras
    completas de Francisco José de Caldas* (Bogotá, 1966), pp. 323–33
Chepstow-Lusty, Alex, 'Agro-pastoralism and Social Change in the
    Cuzco Heartland of Peru: A Brief History using Environmental
    Proxies', *Antiquity*, LXXXV (2011), pp. 570–82
Cobo, Bernabé, *Historia del nuevo mundo* (Seville, 1895)
Crosby, Alfred, *The Columbian Exchange: Biological and Cultural
    Consequences of 1492* (Westport, CT, 1972)
Danson, William, *Alpaca, The Original Peruvian Sheep, Before the
    Spaniards Invaded South America, for Naturalisation in other
    Countries. Recommended through the Natural History Society of
    Liverpool in 1839* (Liverpool, 1852)
Deville, M. E., *Considérations sur les avantages de la naturalisation
    en france de l'alpaca* (Paris, 1851)

Fauvety, Augusto, *Primera introducción de alpacas y llamas en la república oriental del Uruguay* (Montevideo, 1867)

Flannery, Kent, Joyce Marcus and Robert Reynolds, *The Flocks of the Wamani: A Study of Llama Herders on the Punas of Ayacucho, Peru* (San Diego, CA, 1980)

Flores-Ochoa, Jorge, *Pastoralists of the Andes: The Alpaca Herders of Paratía* (Philadelphia, PA, 1979)

Gordon, Iain, ed., *The Vicuña: The Theory and Practice of Community-based Wildlife Management* (New York, 2009)

Kadwell, Miranda, and Jane Wheeler et al., 'Genetic Analysis Reveals the Wild Ancestors of the Llama and the Alpaca', *Proceedings of the Royal Society, London*, 268 (2001), pp. 2575–85

Ledger, Charles, 'The Alpaca', in George Bennett, MD, FLS, *The Third Annual Report of the Acclimatisation Society of New South Wales* (Sydney, 1864), pp. 90–100

MacQuarrie, Kim, *Gold of the Andes: The Llamas, Alpacas, Vicuñas and Guanacos of South America* (Barcelona, 1995)

Markham, Clements R., ed. and trans., *The Travels of Pedro Cieza de León, AD 1532–50, Contained in the First Part of his Chronicle of Peru* (London, 1864)

Mengoni Goñalons, Guillermo Luis, 'Camelids in Ancient Andean Societies: A Review of the Zooarcheological Evidence', *Quaternary International*, CLXXXV (2008), pp. 59–68

Mills, Kenneth, *Idolatry and its Enemies: Colonial Andean Religion and Extirpation, 1640–1750* (Princeton, NJ, 1997)

Molina, Cristóbal de, *Account of the Fables and Rites of the Incas* (Austin, TX, 2011)

Molina, Juan Ignacio, *Compendio de la historia geográfica, natural y civíl del reyno de Chile* (Madrid, 1788)

Monardes, Nicolás, *Primera, segunda y tercera parte de la historia medicina* (Seville, 1574)

Nowak, Katarzyna, 'Legalizing Rhino Horn Trade Won't Save Species, Ecologist Argues. What can South Africa's Rhino Horn Trade Proponents Learn from Experiences with the South American Vicuña?', *National Geographic* (8 January 2015)

Osborne, Michael, *Nature, the Exotic and the Science of French Colonialism* (Bloomington, IN, 1994)

Salomon, Frank, and George L. Urioste, eds and trans, *The Huarochirí Manuscript: A Testament of Ancient and Colonial Andean Religion* (Austin, TX, 1991)

Spalding, Karen, *Huarochirí: An Andean Society under Inca and Spanish Rule* (Stanford, CA, 1984)

Topsell, Edward, *The historie of foure-footed beastes . . . collected out of all the volumes of Conradus Gesner, and all other writers to this present day* (London, 1607)

Torres, Hernán, ed., *South American Camelids: An Action Plan for their Conservation* (Gland, IUCN Species Survival Commission, 1992)

Tristán, Flora, *Peregrinations of a Pariah*, ed. and trans. Jean Hawkes (London, 1986)

Urton, Gary, 'Animals and Astronomy in the Quechua Universe', *Proceedings of the American Philosophical Society*, CXXV/2 (1981), pp. 110–27

Vargas Llosa, Mario, *La Ciudad y los Perros* (Madrid, 2006)

—, *Lituma en los Andes* (Barcelona, 2010)

De la Vega, Garcilaso, *Primera parte de los comentarios reales* (Madrid, 1829)

Walton, William, *A Memoir Addressed to Proprietors of Mountain and other Waste Lands and Agriculturalists of the United Kingdom, on the Naturalisation of the Alpaca* (London, 1841)

—, *The Alpaca: Its Naturalisation in the British Isles Considered as a National Benefit, and as an Object of Immediate Utility to the Farmer and Manufacturer* (New York, 1845)

Warren, Adam, 'From Natural History to Popular Remedy: Animals and Their Medicinal Applications among the Kallawaya in Colonial Peru', in *Centering Animals in Latin American History*, ed. Martha Few and Zeb Tortorici (Chapel Hill, NC, 2014), pp. 123–48

Wheeler, Jane, 'Evolution and Present Situation of the South American Camelidae', *Biological Journal of the Linnaean Society*, LIV (1995), pp. 271–95

Associations and Websites

There are a large number of associations and websites devoted to the breeding and marketing of llamas and alpacas and the conservation of guanacos and vicuñas. The following are just a selection.

ALPACA OWNERS' ASSOCIATION
www.alpacainfo.com
For alpaca owners in North America.

AUSTRALIAN ALPACA ASSOCIATION
www.alpaca.asn.au
Provides advice and contacts for alpaca farmers in Australia.

BRITISH ALPACA SOCIETY
www.bas-uk.com
Website 'dedicated to the welfare of alpacas and the education of their owners in the UK'.

BRITISH CAMELIDS
www.britishcamelids.co.uk
Promotes the responsible ownership, breeding and farming of llamas, alpacas and guanacos in the UK.

BRITISH LLAMA SOCIETY
www.britishllamasociety.org
Offers advice to llama owners in the UK.

INTERNATIONAL ALPACA ASSOCIATION
www.aia.org.pe/en
Founded in Peru to promote the trade in alpaca wool and guarantee
its quality.

INTERNATIONAL CAMELID QUARTERLY
www.llamas-alpacas.com
Magazine featuring the latest news on camelids.

LLAMA ASSOCIATION OF NORTH AMERICA
www.lanainfo.org
For North American llama owners.

MICHELL GROUP
www.michell.com.pe
One of the major producers of alpaca fibre, based in Arequipa, Peru.

SOUTH EAST LLAMA RESCUE
www.southeastllamarescue.org
Rescues unwanted or abused llamas and alpacas in the southeastern
U.S. and puts them up for adoption.

Acknowledgements

I have long been a fan of the llama and its relatives and, over the past two years, many of my friends, family and colleagues have shared my obsession. I am grateful for their enthusiasm and assistance, and hope that I have convinced them that llamas are wonderful things.

Of the countless people who have been kind enough to share their llama knowledge with me, I would like to thank my colleagues (past and present) at the University of York, especially Tara Alberts, Henrice Altink, Sabine Clarke, Laura Crombie, Simon Ditchfield, Joanna de Groot, Catriona Kennedy, David Moon, Tim Smith and Kathleen Walker-Meikle, who have kept me constantly updated on all things llama. I would also like to thank Oliver Hochadel, who passed on valuable information about llamas and alpacas in nineteenth-century Spain; Rebecca Earle, who shared her knowledge of llamas in colonial Peru; and Jorge Meza of Condor Travel, who explained the alpaca wool production process to me at Mundo Alpaca, Arequipa. My parents, Susan and Peter Cowie, and Mari and Gordon Williams, have done a sterling job in supplying me with llama images, books and information, while my sister, Alice Cowie, has shared her expertise in animal behaviour. Staff at Reaktion Books also helped shape and improve my manuscript, particularly Michael Leaman and series editor Jonathan Burt. Above all, my thanks go to Paul Williams, who has accompanied me in search of camelids in Devon, Yorkshire, Spain and Peru, and who took many of the photographs in this book. I hope he still loves llamas as much as I do!

Photo Acknowledgements

The author and publishers wish to express their thanks to the below sources of illustrative material and/or permission to reproduce it:

Alte Pinakothek, Munich (photo © bpk – Bildagentur für Kunst, Kultur und Geschichte, Berlin): p. 74; American Museum of Natural History, New York: p. 42; © ANIMALS by VISION/Alamy: p. 144; Antonini Museum, Nazca, Peru: p. 32; © Archivo y Biblioteca Nacionales de Bolivia, Sucre: p. 103; Archive of Early American Images, The John Carter Brown Library, Brown University, Providence, Rhode Island: p. 73; © Arco Images GmbH/Alamy Stock Photo: p. 11; © BIOSPHOTO/ Alamy: p. 20; author photos: pp. 12, 13, 14, 18, 21, 22, 24, 25, 56, 69, 71, 75 (top left), 101, 104, 128, 129, 134, 136, 137, 138, 140, 142, 143, 146, 147, 148, 149, 150, 153, 156, 162, 164; collection of the author: pp. 15, 16, 19, 23, 26, 83, 85, 88, 91, 96, 98, 99, 107, 109, 111, 123, 127, 132, 147, 150, 152, 155, 163, 165, 198; Carlos Dreyer Museum, Puno, Peru: p. 102; © Oliver Förstner/Alamy: p. 139; Conrad Gessner, *Historia animalium* (Zürich, 1593); © Y. Levy/Alamy: p. 68; Mitchell Library, State Library of New South Wales, Sydney: pp. 97, 116, 117, 130; Museo de América, Madrid: pp. 47, 76; Museo Inca, Cuzco: p. 46; Museo Nacional de Arqueología, Antropología e Historia del Peru, Lima: pp. 29, 30 (top); © Patrimonio Nacional: pp. 79, 92; Pedro Cieza de León, *Primera parte de la crónica del Perú* (Seville, 1553): pp. 52, 75 (top right); private collection: p. 112; Richard Ellis/Getty Images: p. 151; photos © Royal Library of Copenhagen: pp. 36, 37, 43, 44, 59, 70, 80; photo © Tristan Savatier: p. 67; © Victoria and Albert Museum, London: p. 161; photos © The Wellcome

Library, London: pp. 17, 65, 124; The Yale Center for British Art, New Haven, Connecticut: pp. 87, 110.

Index